YORKSH

TRANSVESTITE FOUND DEAD ON EVEREST!

Extremely Unheroic Adventure Writing

Mike Harding

HAYLOFT

First published 2005

Hayloft Publishing Ltd, Kirkby Stephen,
Cumbria, CA17 4DJ

tel: (017683) 42300
fax. (017683) 41568
e-mail: books@hayloft.org.uk
web: www.hayloft.org.uk

ISBN 1 904524 42 7

A catalogue record for this book is available
from the British Library

Printed and bound in the EU

Papers used by Hayloft are natural, recyclable products made from wood
grown in sustainable forests. The manufacturing processes
conform to the environmental regulations of the country of origin.

Jacket illustration by Joe Boske

To Tobias and Felix
with whom I hope to ramble in the mountains one day.

Introduction

For the last eleven years I have taken out my quill and inkhorn on a monthly basis to do battle with the muse, and have produced, each month, a thousand words of gibber to do with mountains and some such for *The Great Outdoors*, a British magazine concerned with trekking, backpacking and walking. My editors, John Manning, (a wool-dyed Yorkshireman) and Cameron McNeish (AKA Macaroon Camiknickers) have done their best to keep me on the straight and relevant and have failed.

Gathered between these covers, dear reader, is a selection of those articles, the demented ramblings of a lapsed Catholic of no particular mountaineering ability who has found himself at various times: on the flanks of Mount Everest, in the belly of the Hindu Kush, and in the tea rooms under Hardcastle Crags.

None of this has done me much harm, and may even have done me some good. At least I can claim to be the first comedian to have been to both Everest and K2, as well as Splot and Oswaldtwhistle. I can also claim to be the first European to cross the Gangalwat Pass in Northern Pakistan, and probably the last, since it was bloody hard and there wasn't a lot to see.

As a result of all this walking and trekking I now know where some of the places are that Wild Bill Whalley talked about in O Level Joggers in St. Bede's, Manchester, all those aeons ago.

In the lines of the immortal Virgil,

'*Maxima via est quid non radix habet.*' [1]

Mike Harding,
Connemara,
2005

[1] *It's a long road that has no turnips.*

The Sahib with the Exploding Trousers

I suppose it may be something entirely personal though I doubt it: dried apricots I mean. 'Energy food,' a woman in the know who writes the health bits in *The Great Outdoors* magazine opined the other month, 'Stock up with them for those long days out in the hills, and whenever you feel the old blood sugar level sink, then get your laughing tackle round a dried apricot, and all will be well. The blood sugar level will zoom up and you will do a Linford Christie up the north face of Umigooly.'

Well I believed her. So much so that on my last trek in Pakistan I bought a stone of dried apricots from a Hunza lady for something like two bob, merrily munching them as I left the village behind and headed across the arid dusty desert wastes towards the glacier that was to be my home for the next month. Lovely they tasted, naturally sweet with lots of flavour. Rightfully are the apricots of Hunza prized. More virtuous than rubies are they, and is it not written that Alexander the Great had four elephants set aside solely for the task of carrying the looted apricots he nicked back to his gaff in Alexandria?

But dried apricots don't suit everybody. To Alexander and his missus they may have been an innocuous and beneficial little snack with no harmful side effects whatsoever. Other people – and I gentle reader am one of them – have a strange reaction to the dried version of the fruit. I don't know whether it is because the stomach has to work double hard to re-hydrate the fibres of the apricot, and then has to work triple hard to make all the enzymes that will break the flesh of the fruit down to release the essential sugars, or whether there is some essential fructic acid in the cellular composition of the apricot that reacts with the zygotes or whatever you call 'em in a non carminative way .

To be honest I haven't a clue, and even worse I don't give a chuff what the scientific reason is. All I know is that at the end of day one of the apricot diet I was known to the Baltistani porters as, *The Sahib With The Exploding Trousers.*

High altitude flatulence, like high altitude oedema is something all of us who go to the mountains experience from time to time, and at first I simply put the fact that my rear end was behaving like a 650cc Kawasaki being kick started on an icy morning, down to the effects of altitude. After a few days when the porters were stopping after every cannonade to drop their loads, and roll in the dust helpless with laughter, it struck me, old Himalayan hand that I was, that there may be something more to the matter, particularly since the eruptions were prefaced by severe griping pains and the feeling that somebody had shoved the nozzle of a bike pump through my navel and was trying to inflate me.

It was almost a week before it dawned on me that it was the apricots what did it, by which time the porters were weak from laughter, and my tent flaps were in shreds. Vango Force Tens are designed to withstand gales from without, not sudden massive increases of air pressure from within, and for the rest of the trek the zip on the door was replaced by a series of safety pins.

I know this isn't a very nice subject for an article, but I speak out mainly in the hope that those of you likewise tempted by the apricot diet will first of all try it out in the privacy of your own home where the worst that can happen is that you will deafen the cat, or blow the feathers off the canary. As I say, I pass this information on simply in the light of our common humanity.

Talking of Pakistan, I have been fractious to the point of being nangy recently, to such an extent that the two cats who share the house with me have taken to checking out what mood I'm in before they enter the room. This is because I am suffering from Long Trek Withdrawal Syndrome. It is two years since I packed my crampons and folding sink in my kit bag, flew in an aluminium tube to the Indian subcontinent, left a road head behind, and set off into the fairly unknown with a gaggle of porters, and enough food for a month to scramble my way round somewhere hot and dusty that leads to somewhere cold and icy, and I am feeling the loss terribly.

The last time I was out in the Himalayas I stayed out for three and a half months and loved every minute of it, apart from the terrible air pollution in Kathmandu.

Oh but I do miss the mountains: waking in the morning with a mug of 'bed tea' and the cheerful voices of the kitchen lads as they shout, 'Good Morning Sahib, good weather today'; I miss the genuine smiles of the porters who start off as strangers and rapidly become friends. I miss the mountains of course, the stunning beauty and raw majesty of the snow covered ranges; and I miss the Buddhist temples with the scent of burning juniper twigs and the chants of the monks at puja. Most of all I miss the silence, the peace that is to be found in the mountains, the knowledge that you are days away from any road and any sign of what society would have us believe is the civilised world.

So I've taken out the maps and the guides and started working out a trek or two that I might fit in – if the day job allows, tracing possible and impossible routes in the mountains, wondering who fancies coming with me and what it will all be like. I can already smell the burning juniper and hear the hollow booming of the gongs and the thudding drums of the temples. And with the help of God and a few policemen, this time there will be no barking trousers, because I'm sticking to Kendal Mint Cake.

March, 1999

Vicar has Sex in Matchbox

There's some kind of anniversary of the Scouting movement coming up: the three hundredth anniversary of the invention of the woggle or something, and because of this I was invited to take part in a BBC Radio programme recently, in which various people talked about their experiences as Boy Sprouts. Having recorded stand-up comedy routines about cubs and scouts and beans laced with paraffin and their effect on the digestive system of small boys, the producer decided that I would be suitable microphone fodder, and dragged me into a studio to gibber about my experiences. Any reference to certain Scout Leaders having at times had a propensity for examining the personal bits of small boys in their charge was rubbed out electronically even though I was very discreet and only referred to one occasion when, at camp in Devon, our Scoutmaster had insisted on examining me every night on account of a small patch of heat rash. The phrase, 'Let's have another look at that rash of yours' still rings in my ear as one of those Proustian keys that can send the hands of the clock spinning back through the years.

Ah the joys of lying under canvas staring out at the lashing rain, looking forward to cooking dampers and twists over a sulky wood fire. I can still taste them in my mind's mouth even after all these years: raw flour dough rolled into a long worm, twisted round a stick and cooked over an open fire. It was like eating a smoke pasty. The Scout Leader who invented that little bit of backwoods cuisine was probably drummed out of the Inquisition for cruelty.

After the TV debacle I found myself working as a childminder. Not that I have changed career in mid-life and opened a creche or anything like that; it's just that my sister and her better half won a holiday to Africa, and left the kids behind: Elicia, a small blond mini fuhrer of two and three quarters, and Alex, a blond

Manchester United fan of almost, nearly, soon-to-be eight arrived in the Dales to stay with Uncle Mike. Since they spend most of their small lives in Crumpsall, that place of dark Satanic Cream Cracker Biscuit Factories where I was born and brung up, it seemed a good idea to take them out on a short walk or two to show them that the countryside isn't something with a bandstand at one end and a bowling green at the other, or something with red flags stuck all over it and men with sticks hitting little white things into holes in the ground.

The walks were eventful and have now gained me full membership of the *Hansel and Gretel Parents School of Walking* and the *Curmudgeon's Child Rearing Club.* Elicia can ask more questions than a Witchfinder General, while Alex has more energy than is good for any child, and makes me understand why the Victorians were so keen to harness this kind of stuff, and sent children down the mines and up chimneys where they belong. Elicia is going through the phrase known as the Terrible Twos and her main hobby (when she isn't asking questions) is contradicting everything and everyone.

'Time for a walk now. Are we putting our trainers on?' was followed by, 'I don't like walking.'

'Oh yes you do,' was followed by, 'No I don't.'

With the sort of low cunning normally reserved for Jesuits I worked out a way of winning in this kind of argument.

'You don't want to go for a walk on this lovely sunny day and see the cows and chickens and sheep,' I said.

'Yes I do anyway,' she shouted with the bottom lip sticking out like a saucer ('anyway' meaning the same thing as definitely in her lexicon).

Off we went through lovely, sunny Dentdale, birds singing, sheep doing sheep stuff, and cows quietly wondering whether they were mad, with Alex already a small spot in the distance and Elicia asking me where the sheep's mummies were. This seems to be something she is going through at the moment, everything that moves: cats, worms, chickens, buses, etc., have mummies, and where the mummies are is very important.

'The sheep's mummies are at home making the tea,' I lied. (Actually they could have been for all I know.)

'What are they having for tea?'

'Grass – with mint sauce,' I added, compounding the felony.

'Yuk! I don't like grass. It's full of sex.'

'What do you mean, sex?'

'Capertillars and heardwigs and beekles.'

'They are insects.'

'No they're not they are sex.'

I remembered a vicar in Crumpsall who once showed me a rare moth he had caught and put in a matchbox, and momentarily saw, in my mind's eye, the headline in the *News of the World*, Vicar Has Sex in Matchbox, but dismissed it before it did my brain any permanent harm. A little further on we watched a herd of cows grazing on the lush summer grass. One of them dumped a load of good for the roses on the ground.

'How do cows wipe their bottoms?'

'I don't know.'

'Why?'

'Because I never asked them.'

'Why don't they wear nappies?'

'Because they're too expensive.'

'Oh. Where are their mummies?'

'Making tea. And for tea they are having cheese on toast and a milk shake.'

'Strawberry or banana?'

'Banana.'

'Do cows have willies?'

'Some of them do.'

'That cow's got lots of willies.'

'No that's the cow's udder. That's where milk comes from.'

'No that's lots of willies. Milk comes from Tescos.'

I now understood why Alex was half way up the hill singing,

'Ooh ah Cantona,
Wears frilly knickers and his girlfriend's bra.'

He obviously has a lot of this to put up with. When I finally got back to the house, having carried Elicia the last mile because she had, 'A bone in my leg,' I decided to have a medal struck for her parents for when they come back from Africa. If they come back. Perhaps they too have joined the Hansel and Gretel School of Parenting, and were wise enough to drop a trail of bread crumbs all the way to the plane steps when they were leaving.

August, 1997

Yorkshire Transvestite Found Dead on Everest

I was musing the other day on the North South Divide. Ask not the reason why – that is our job as columnists: to muse. We even take special musing courses at country mansions in Wiltshire that have now been converted into management training centres. A week after the fat men in the grey suits have gone home wrecked from seven days of trying to build rafts out of fence posts and chicken wire with which they cross a river in flood; or traversing minefields at dark of night carrying an egg in a condom, in we come with our bottles of single malt and our green eye shades to do a week's intensive musing. However I digress.

So there I was, musing on the North South thingy, on the fact that all the mountains and hills are in the north, and all the flat bits are in the south. The line that Wild Bill Whalley, our joggers teacher at Stallag Kinder St Bede's, Manchester, taught us about, that runs from Bristol to the Wash is not just a fig tree of the imagination, it is something tangible and real. Bill Bryson in his meanderings about our planet, for all that he is one astute Yank – an endangered species – missed out completely on the fact that the land of cloth caps and whippets, and the land of jellied eels, pearly kings and queens and Dick Van Dyke accents are chalk and cheese, and never the twain shall meet.

Of course from time to time in my travels I have met ex-pat northerners living in places like Stevenage New Town and Basildon who assure me, as they put their pints of Old Clenchbuttock down on the polished bar of the Frog and Flymo, that, 'the south isn't all that bad, once you get used to it'. But I can tell by the dullness in their eyes that this is a mantra they have rehearsed far too many times for it to have the slightest ring of truth.

The fact is that the north has the mountains, and mountains make us different people. All right, they are hardly on the scale of the Hindu Kush or the Pamirs, but at two thousand feet plus they will do. From Mid and North Wales to the fierce wilds of Cape Wrath lovely mountain after mountain calls us up it with the clarion call of the Great Beyond, and lads and lasses of sinewy thew and hearty hearts have for yonks been pulling on their shorts and stuffing their ruckers for a day on the hill, untrammelled by the noises of coughing whippets and the cries of small children as they are sent yet again down the dark mine or under the chattering looms up at t'Mill (this is what happens when you wax your lyricals).

And it is this, this closeness to the mountains that has made Northern Men and Women what they are today: the salt, pepper and chip butties of the Earth. All the Great Men And Women Of The World came from the north or if they didn't – they wish they had done. Captain Cook came from Whitby, and if it hadn't been for him the Aborigines would never have known that they were living in Australia, and would have been all confused. The computer was invented at Manchester University, and Take That and Oasis both come from that fair city while Liverpool of course had the Beatles, and it is a little-known truth that Adolph Hitler spent his summer holidays at New Brighton, and that is just to mention a few things off the top of my head. Oh, and it's also a little known fact that Arthur Parrot, who was the first man to have the idea of burying cats up to their eyeballs in the middle of the road so that cars could find their way home in the dark, was a Barnsley lighthouse keeper.

Which brings me in a roundabout way to the nub of my argument – Maurice Wilson.

Maurice Wilson is one of the great unsung heroes of Himalayan mountaineering, and a Yorkshireman to boot. It's not often that you will hear a Lancastrian like myself saying good things about a Yorkshireman, but in the cause of Northern Solidarity little things like the fact that Lancashire is better at everything must be put to one side for a moment. All of the following is absolutely true and can be checked via Google, *The Encyclopedia Britannica* and the British Library.

Maurice Wilson was born plain Maurice Wilson in the dying years of the nineteenth century. As a mere lad he volunteered for the army in the First World War, and was sent to the trenches where, at the battle of Ypres, he suffered the most atrocious machine gun wounds. While recovering from his wounds he contacted TB and, on the edge of a total physical and mental breakdown, managed to cure himself by fasting and prayer. (It takes more than a few Hun bullets and TB to kill a Yorkshireman).

Reasoning that God had spared him for greater things, Wilson decided to climb Everest without oxygen. The fact that he had never climbed anything higher than Stoodley Pike in his life deterred him not one whit, and he set about planning his expedition in meticulous detail. He decided to fly to Tibet, crash land his plane on the Rongbuk Glacier, and simply walk to the top of the mountain sustained by nothing more than his belief that faith could do anything. The fact that he couldn't fly and had no plane didn't bother him either. He bought a second hand Gypsy Moth, christened it *Ever Wrest* and signed up for flying lessons at the London Aero Club.

The Air Ministry together with the various countries whose permission he needed to fly over sent telegrams telling him that he should stay in Yorkshire, and fly nothing but his pigeons. Wilson tore up all the telegrams, and flew by a circuitous route to Darjeeling where he hired three native porters, disguised himself as a local by rubbing walnut juice into his skin and, dressed in native clothes, set off for the mountain.

From then on his luck seems to have dried up. He reached the foot of the mountain and began the climb, at which point the porters, realising that he was a Yorkshireman, deserted him. According to received wisdom he died of hypothermia and exhaustion while trying to climb the ice chimney onto the North Col some time in June 1934.

It is here that the story takes on a character more mysterious than any *Da Vinci Code*, since the first people to come across Wilson's body and his diaries were Eric Shipton and Dan Bryant while on the Everest expedition of 1935. Shipton was not just a southerner but was also a Northophobe. Are we to believe him when he tells us that amongst Maurice Wilson's personal belongings were items of women's clothing, and writings that show him to have been a fetishist? Are we to believe him – this man who would do an expedition of three months on only one shirt (at least Yorkshireman wash once a month!) when he tells us that some of these items of clothing were, and I quote, 'intimate items'?

I put it to you ladies and gentlemen of the jury that the truth is something far far different from that Kleenex of lies that has been sold to us down the years by Shipton and Co. I believe that Maurice Wilson did make it to the summit of Everest and that Shipton sought to conceal the fact. The women's clothing – well even if it were true, everybody has to have a hobby. In any case, is it not possible that Wilson, being a true northerner, was doing Everest the hardest way possible: in sling backs, liberty bodice and cami-knickers?

Can you see what a scoop this would be? The headlines in the newspapers of Merry England (and remember this was 1935) would have read, *Everest Climbed By Yorkshire Transvestite – King To Give Him/Her Knighthood!!*

Transvestite? I think not and smell all the nastiness of yet another Southern Plot.

January 1998

We're Open when we're Closed

People imagine that mega media stars like myself spend all our time when not at the VDU and keyboard out at Langam's Brassiere and Marco Pier White's with one or other of the Spice Matrons on our arms. Not so. In the interests of Great Outdoor Journalism and Research we spend whatever free time we get, up to our armpits in slutch and peat bog, being attacked by midges and frost bite, or in the most severe cases frost-bitten midges. Thus it was that I found myself, in the cause of great writing, yet again on the boat from Stranraer to Larne heading out for Sligo and Donegal.

It wasn't the best time of year for walking in the west of Ireland – winter not yet gone and spring not yet arrived – the Limbo time when earth is still brown and dead, and the days are only just beginning to have lighter streaks of grey in them. Still, I needed to recharge my emotional batteries, and with banjo, boots and Blarney-repellent cream I was soon off the B and I ferry scooting through Enniskillen towards the west.

It was just across the border in the Republic that I had another of my subliminal experiences. I have these in the way other people have dandruff or belly button fluff. A subliminal experience? Well it's a sort of happening, a bit like being abducted by aliens, or assumed into Heaven (so that's what happened to the Virgin Mary – she was abducted by aliens!); the sort of thing that nobody believes is true when you tell them about it.

Such as, just before Christmas when I'm on my way to deliver a pair of Loch Fyne kippers to two gay American poets in a car full of dobros, concertinas, hammered dulcimers and bowed psalteries. Half way down the back lane in Dentdale, I hit a flood and the car engine explodes, leaving me to wade through Y-front deep muddy water looking for rescue. When it arrives in the shape of a pick-up truck I compliment the driver on his route finding: me being stuck in a remote flood down a remote lane, in a remote Yorkshire Dale, and him coming from Penrith.

'I used to do a lot of bonking in this lane,' he told this distressed column as it stood there with its shoes round its neck, and its trousers rolled up to its arm pits. Then, as he hauled the car onto the truck, and the gay American poets wondered where their kippers were, he gave me a blow by grunt account of his early love life acted out on bucolic summer evenings in the then not flooded lane. That's what I mean by a subliminal experience.

South of the Irish Border it was a little more demure and circumspect, though not half of one jot less surreal. The car (mended now with a new engine) was filthy (cow muck, sheep wool, mud and dust) and I decided that, since I was going on my holidays, it should have a wash.

Driving through the Free State Irish Republic rain I noticed a garage with a sign saying 'Hand Car Wash Here!!' and pulled in. The car wash with its brushes and hoses and hot wax finish seemed still and moribund. It was raining. It was glum as a bucket. I was glum as a bucket. You would have been glum as several buckets. Even the Dalai Lama would have been as glum as half a bucket. Then a glum man who had been watching me from a glum doorway detached himself from it, and came glumly towards me through the glum rain.

'The car wash is closed,' he said with an overtone of glum.

'Oh bugger,' said I.

'But I'll give it a hand wash for you if you like,' he said, and he vanished, only to reappear with a bucket (not glum) and brush and a hose pipe full of hot water.

'Do you want the full job?' he asked.

'Yes,' I said.

'Well get yourself a cup of coffee over there,' he said, nodding towards a café.

'It looks closed,' I said.

'It is,' he said. 'But she'll make you a cup of coffee anyway.'

And the lady who ran the closed café made a cup of fresh filter coffee for me, and gave me a nice buttered scone.

And when I asked the man who had washed my car how much he wanted he said, 'Whatever you think,' and I paid him twice what the car wash would have cost me.

'Thank you for that,' I said. 'Do you do a lot of this?'

'Only when the car wash is closed,' he said.

'What do you do the rest of the week?'

'I run the car wash, and the wife runs the café. We're only licensed for six days. So we're not open today.'

'So I didn't have a car wash and a coffee and scone at all.'

'That's right sir, you did not, and if you go down the road there's a supermarket that isn't open where you can get a newspaper.'

I arrived in Sligo with just enough daylight left to climb Knocknarea, a simple climb up the great hill where, according to legend, Queen Maeve lies slumbering under a massive cairn. And something very strange happened while I was climbing. As I reached the summit I could have sworn that I heard music in the air. Nothing I could define, something like the far off sound of a flute or whistle coming and going in the light wind.

There are lots of stories in Ireland of music coming from out of the sides of hills or mountains: The Gold Ring, Paddy's Rambles In The Park, and Port nab Pucai (The Fairies' Jig) from the Blaskett Islands are such magical tunes. Archaeologists have suggested that this may be something to do with the fact that the earliest people here, the legendary Firbolg who dwelt mostly in the hills and mountains, built their houses out of stone and covered them with turf, creating fougous and souterrains as secret ways in and out. After a few years the houses would simply look like grassy mounds, and would seem to be part of the hillside. It is easy to imagine some proto-Celt in County Kerry wandering back from dancing round the nipples of Anu falling asleep on some such a hump, full of barley cake and beer, waking in the night to hear music coming from under the earth courtesy of the

Firbolg Arms Karaoke Night.

But whether the music I heard was spirit music, or existed out there in the real world, (somebody down below perhaps practising the tin whistle) I'll never know. And it hardly matters anyway, since there is music of another kind here: the music that you only find in solitude and remoteness, the music the wind makes in the grass, the music a lark makes as it rises off its nest, and the music in the soul that is born of freedom, and the music of closed car washes that are open and shut cafés that serve coffee and scones.

March, 1998

The Devil's Bollocks

I've spent most of this summer walking in the west of Ireland, everywhere from Donegal in the north to Mizen Head in the far south. It's wonderful walking country, ranging from wild and woolly hills like the Maumturks of Connemara, to gentler stuff in the karst country of the Burren. But what fascinated me as much as the raw beauty of the Irish hills was the fact that everywhere I walked I was treading on stories: every hill, every pass, every col or cwm has a story attached to it, and if you can't find it in a book, then the locals will have it off by heart. The whole hill country of the west is just one long epic narrative.

A couple of years back, I climbed Knocknarea in Sligo on a lovely June day. Not a soul on the top just myself, a couple of rabbits, and the burial mound of Queen Maeve, a great white rubble cairn under which lies the remains of the most powerful woman in mythic Ireland, Maeve. She seems to have been a sort of Celtic version of Maggie Thatcher with the humility cut out. Lying in bed with her spouse one night she began an argument as to who had the most worldly goods. This was in the days when, under Celtic law, a woman's possessions remained hers after marriage. It turned out that Maeve and her hubby were neck and neck except for a great bull that her husband owned. Hearing that there was another, far more wonderful bull belonging to Cuchulain over in Cooley, Maeve sent off her army to capture it and the famous Cattle Raid of Cooley took place, the *Tain Bó Coolaigh* remembered in one of the earliest Irish epic poems. And there I was, stood on the hill where the great woman's bones were buried, just me and a couple of rabbits.

A few weeks later in County Cork I walked the Goughane Barra Horseshoe. It was a stinking foul day with grey leaden clouds the colour of old soggy flannel vests hanging about the mountains at about a thousand feet above sea-level, so that for most of the day I was stumbling through bogs and up crags in next to zero visibility. As I was descending towards a narrow pass called Poll, the cloud lifted, and the land below me was suddenly slashed with bars of bright sunlight. Poll was the scene of one of the great escapes of the Irish War of Independence when Major Tom Barry, led by a local man who had cobbled together a long rope from odds and ends, brought his IRA flying column over from Cumhalla into Goughane Barra to escape encirclement and capture. His book *Guerrilla Days in Ireland* is a first hand account of the Irish armed struggle that led to Independence.

'For over an hour,' he writes, 'man after man with the aid of stretched out rifles and that useful rope, swung and slithered down that rough passage to the level ground of Goughane Barra.' Peering down into the slimy stone staircase of Poll this day it was hard to see how anybody could have climbed that in black night, much less got to the bottom in one piece.

Stories within stories, stories in the stone.

When the weather is too poor to get up on to the tops there is still plenty of good walking to be had in Ireland. The back roads are quiet enough to be safe in the main, and there are woodland walks and coastal paths in plenty.

One Sunday morning in spring I took such a walk out of Sligo with a few sandwiches, a map and not much else. The weather was biting cold and grey, just the kind of day you wouldn't want to be up on Benbulbin or over in the Ox Mountains. I took the Lough Gill road out of town with hardly a soul about, rambled past the holy well at Tobernalt, and walked around the lake to Dooney Rock. Everywhere you go in Sligo the poetry of W. B. Yeats whistles through your mind like a wind.

Dooney Rock is where the fiddler in the poem came from who has a brother and a cousin who are priests. But even though he is only a fiddler he will be invited through the door of Heaven first...

For the good are always merry,
Save by an evil chance,
And the merry love the fiddle,
And the merry love to dance:

And when the folk there spy me,
They will all come up to me,
With 'Here is the fiddler of Dooney!'
And dance like a wave of the sea.

Bits and pieces like that you can find in the books, but at other times local people will give you the stories that lie under the earth and stones. The first time I climbed the Devil's Mother in Mayo it was on a foul, wet blustery day that changed suddenly to brilliant blue skies and a drying wind. Such a change is common in Ireland where weather of any kind rarely lasts long.

Afterwards in the Leenaun Heritage Centre I asked Michael who runs the place, why the hill was called the Devil's Mother expecting there to be some tale of Old Nick and immortal souls bargained for.

'Ah, that was because of the British army,' he said. 'When the sappers were mapping the hills roundabout a local man told them the name in Irish, *Maigairli an Deamhain*. 'What does that mean?' asked the sapper, and your man, wanting to spare him embarrassment said, 'the Devil's Mother'. But it really means The Devil's Bollocks.'

I looked it up that night in the dictionary. He was right. And how did it get the name? Ah now, that's another story entirely.

October, 1995

Ju Ju and Magnetic North

I have always been deeply suspicious of Magnetic North. How can you trust something that moves about so much? I remember as a boy scout how shaken I was to find that True North and the North that my shaking compass needle pointed towards were not one and the same thing. I was more distressed than I had been when I discovered that it was my dad and not Father Christmas who bumbled in breathing beer fumes all over the bedroom on Christmas Eve, to cack-handedly stuff the Rupert Book, the Broons Annual and the rubber dagger in my pillow case.

We did map-reading one Friday night in the cold and dusty school hall where our scout troop met. Our scout master, Father Anthony, placed map and compass on the floor before us.

'That,' he said, 'is True North, the North of the grid lines of the map, and that is Magnetic North, the North your compass needle points to – and it changes every year.'

'Why?' I asked innocently.

'Harding!' he shouted, shaking and purple of gill. 'You always want to know the ins and outs of the cat's behind. Last week you asked me why a Granny Knot was called that when your granny couldn't tie one, and the week before you asked me what was the use of learning what a wildebeest spoor looks like when you aren't going to see one at camp in Hardcastle Crags. I despair with you sometimes boy! Magnetic North changes because the Good Lord wants it to, and it's your job as a Catholic boy scout to remember that it shifts, find out where it's shifted to, and re-align your map accordingly. Now O'Toole, Fox Patrol, looking at this map of Morecambe and Lancaster, give me a grid reference for a good camp site with running water and a woods nearby for firewood.'

O'Toole was not the brightest Patrol Leader in the history of the

Scout movement, and gave a bearing that would have had us camping in the middle of Morecambe Bay. Father Anthony went off to take some tablets and lie down, while Skip finished the lesson.

All these years on I still mistrust Magnetic North, particularly since I no longer believe in God, and therefore have even less of an idea why the damn thing wanders about so much. So last month I was fascinated to discover that you can buy things that will give you an accurate fixing by using signals from satellites. I'd only come across such things before on boats when crewing a friend's yacht around the Western Isles. There I was, one black summer's afternoon in a Force Eight under the cliffs of Mull, hanging over the side, emerald of face and blanche of knuckle, feeding the fishes with re-cycled porridge, while Ronnie, the skipper, told me not to worry as he wittered on about the wonders of something called what sounded like 'Dekkar' that could give him his position to an accuracy of thirty metres.

While I was impressed by his description of something that had finally got one over on that tricksy fly-by-night, Magnetic North, I was more concerned with the fact that the horizon, when it could be seen at all, was more often as near vertical as dammit. I prayed to St Christopher, hoping that even though the Pope had downsized him into an honourable or a blessed, or even a plain mister, he could still see his way to getting us out of this mess. I might not believe in God but the odd bit of Ju Ju can still come in handy.

We did get back in one piece, and I forgot all about sailing and such things as satellite navigation for a long time. Then my friend Bill O'Connor showed me this thing he's got that is about the size of a mobile phone that can tell you where you are to within a dozen or so metres. It all looked very flash with lots of buttons to press and an LED thingy and LCD whatsit, and it certainly seemed to do away with sneaky Magnetic North. I consulted it and it told me that I was sitting in Bill's House, but stopped short of telling me that we were in the little room with the fire and the books in it drinking Darjeeling tea.

I was well impressed, as you can imagine, and almost rushed out to buy one straight away. But then a few things bubbled to the surface of my mind like carp coming up for lumps of bread in a monastery pond. What if the batteries run out? And what if the satellite you're using for your fix suddenly does a Hubble on you and goes AWOL. Where are you then? At least with a compass, unless you're in amongst a lot of magnetite, you've got some idea where you are.

And what use would satellite navigation have been to me on top of Mweelrea in Mayo last year when I was in thick mist on a pretty dicey ridge with lots of nothing all around me? I needed something accurate to three feet not thirty metres. In fact what I needed was St Christopher and a chair lift. However I digress.

Bill did confess that most of the time he uses a standard compass and some beads on a string that he uses to count off his paces when he gets stuck in mist. He showed me them – they were rather like those worry beads that Greek men play with while they sit drinking coffee watching their wives and mothers digging the roads and sledge-hammering rocks, wearing thick black dresses in the kind of sun that could roast a tortoise in four minutes. Then I realised that Bill's beads reminded me of something else: the Pundits of Northern India. They played a major part in mapping the Himalayas during the days of The Great Game, disguising themselves as holy men and pilgrims as they were passing through hostile territory, using their beads to count the distance, and their pilgrims' staffs and some pre-O-level trigonometry to gauge the mountains' heights – they mapped most of Northern India, Afghanistan and Pakistan this way.

Well if it's good enough for the Pundits it's good enough for me. So, armed with some rosary beads, a brush stale, and the knowledge that lichen only grows on the north side of trees, I can eschew compass, Magnetic North and satellite navigation for ever. I've just remembered though that there are no trees on top of Mweelrea. I'll have to carry one, a small one.

February, 1997

It's No Go the Laureate

So that's it then! Passed over for the New Year's Honours List yet again: no MBE, no OBE, no Lord Hardinge of Crumpsall. Maybe next year.

Only joking. My socialist antecedents would be spinning in their graves at the mere thought of me tagging anything with the word *'Empire'* on it after my name. Who would be proud of labelling themselves with something that was built on the backs of stolen lands, and enslaved and exploited millions? You might as well tag *Union Carbide* or *Ku Klux Klan* after your name.

And there's no chance of a job as Poet Laureate because Andrew Bowel Movement has got his *gluteus maximus* firmly planted on the Royal Poetry Cushion. Shame really, because I always thought I'd make a good royal poet.

But surely, they've got so many hangers on up there in the upper echelons that another one wouldn't make any difference. I know that Prince Charles and the Duke of Edinburgh both read *The Great Outdoors* magazine – so Phil and Charlie have a deck at the following, bin old Motion, and let this new lad in. He is the voice of the streets – innit? He knows how the yoof of today walk the walk! Give him a job and some bling to flog – now!

THE RAMSBOTTOMS AT GRIMCASTLE CRAGS

There's a famous North Country place called Grimcastle
As is famous for its beetling crags,
And Mr. and Mrs. Ramsbottom
Went there wi' young Albert their lad.

They'd hiking shorts, boots and Gore-Tex cagoules,
Paste sandwiches and bottles of pop,
And a stick with an horse's head handle,
Dad had nicked from the YHA shop.

They rambled up t'bank of the river
Admiring the scenery about,
And mother was washing her trotters in t'watter
When they suddenly heard a loud shout.

'Just what do you think you are doing?'
A right posh voice did call
And the Ramsbottoms looked – a red face and tweed cap
Were skennin' at em over t' wall.

'We're gooin' fer a walk,' said Father.
'A walk?' said the head loud and shrill.
'Aye – walking,' said father. 'It's when yer legs move.
It's quite different from just standing still.'

'In fact all of us Ramsbottoms
Are somewhat adept at the craft,
You could say walking runs in our family.'
Little Albert stifled a laugh.

By now the head were proper blazing
'Cos it knew that the mick were being took,
'Well you can't walk here, it's all private land
So beggar orf!! Go on, sling your hook!'

‘Private?’ said Mother, ‘Who owns it?’
‘I do,’ said the head coming round the wall.
‘And pray sir,’ said mother drying her trotters,
‘Where did you buy it at all?

‘Did you go to a shop where they sell things,
Like rivers and mountains and hills,
And ask for some crags and a river and some trees
Saying, *You can put it all on my bill.*’

‘It was left me by my father,’ the stranger replied,
‘Every sod, every puddle, every stick.
It’s been handed down since the first Lord Grimcastle
Was at Hastings in 1066.’

‘A Ramsbottom fought at Hastings,’ said Father,
‘One of the archers he were,
He had a bad squint and St Vitus’ dance
So his arrers tended to go everywhere.

‘Harold were reviewing his archers
When a sergeant at arms gave a shout,
Prithee sire keep away from Ramsbottom,
He’ll have some poor bugger’s eye out.’

‘And how did the first of your lot get this land?’ asked Ma,
‘He fought for it,’ Grimcastle replied.
Mother stripped right down to her liberty bodice,
‘Right I’ll fight thee for it!’ she cried.

And in the spirit of the fighting Ramsbottoms
Mother fetched Lord Grimcastle a whack
With the stick with the horse’s head handle
And laid the titled pratt out flat.

And that's how the Ramsbottoms got Grimcastle Crags
And little Albert became quite a toff,
Now he wanders the grounds with his horse's head stick
Telling t'ramblers to bugger off.

And Albert has got himself knighted
With a title and a couple of OBEs,
And he prats about in ermine and white tights,
With a garter worn just below the knee.

There's a moral to this tale of course,
Since now to the finish I've come:
Remember, the higher a social monkey climbs,
The more it shows its bum.

So that's it. I now await the knock on the door. It will either be from the Palace offering me Old Bowel Movement's job or MI5 wanting to stick burning matches down my fingernails while they ask me about that trip I made to the Hindu Kush in 1997. And that as they say, is another story entirely.

January, 2003

Dib Dib Dib Dub Dub Dub

I am a great believer in Charles Dickens' maxim that children must be made miserable in their earliest years, otherwise they will never understand that the World is out to get them big style, and that things can only get slightly better – perhaps – maybe. It is for this reason that I take children camping whenever I can.

Let me expound: Oliver Twist and the gruel, Pip Pirrip and the file and wittles, Nicholas Nickleby and Dotheboys Hall – all this misery is good for them. It teaches them that Life is Crap, and makes them appreciate the good times when, and, if they eventually arrive. So it is that camping and its attendant joys: flies, rain, cold, smells, latrine pits and lousy food, is enough to convince any child who is not a masochist that, once they are in some small way in charge of their own destinies, they will spend every holiday they can getting fat on burgers, fries, ice cream and coke by a hotel pool somewhere very warm and very dry.

There will be the hairy chested amongst you reading this now who will be roaring scornfully, 'Botal Tollocks! I went camping for years with the cubs and the scouts – made a man of me! Loved every minute of it!'

It is a little known fact that the cubs and scouts were (notice I use the past tense) paramilitary organisations set up to train young men to be fit guardians of the Empire – which is probably why we lost it. In those days, when half the map was pink, and God had been to Eton, it was every boy's duty to learn how to be kind but stern to little black people while you robbed them of their tea, coffee, ivory, gold, oil, diamonds and rubber. As part of this you had to learn the other stuff about cooking smoke pasties, and sucking pebbles to keep your mouth moist while you followed the spoor of some animal or other, thus gaining the admiration of native people's all over the world. (*Bwana* actually means, *white man who sucks rocks and walks staring at wildebeest shit.*)

It was with my future prospects as a rubber plantation manager in the Congo in mind that my mother enrolled me in the Cub Scout Pack of St. Dunstan The Aggressive, Crumpsall, Manchester. Now in those days we were not over endowed with the mazoola. The family fortunes took a nose dive during the Irish Potato Famine and have been snuffling round the bottom ever since. A proper cub's uniform therefore was out of the question. In fact we didn't even know what the question was.

My mother though was a woman of infinite resources and decided to make me a uniform. She knitted me a green jersey, and made me some shorts by cutting down an old pair of '*shorts, khaki, desert, men's, large, pairs one*' that my Uncle Harry had brought back from his war with Rommel in North Africa. She cut the legs down, but not the bum bit, so that, when I ran, a yard and a half of khaki flapped behind me like a sail and, when I stopped, the loose cloth jumped and doodled around me like a deflated but eager puppy. The knitted boots likewise were not a success.

Still I enjoyed those early days: learning how to recognise different kinds of trees should we ever see any, and learning how to cook for ourselves while we were on the trail. The haute cuisine à la cub sprout was the twist or smoke pasty. You mixed flour and water with a pinch of salt, rolled it into a long snake, twisted it round a green stick and then burned it over a wood fire. This we did in what passed for the African veldt – the field behind the presbytery. There were no wildebeest in Crumpsall in those days, so we followed a dog until it turned nasty and started showing its teeth.

After three weeks of basic training I could eat a smoke pasty, recognise an oak leaf if it ever happened that I saw one, and would certainly know a wildebeest if one ever got loose on the streets of Manchester.

Thus armed they took us Sons of The Empire to camp at Whittle Le Woods, Chorley, in the grounds of a big pub that was run by a bloke what our Akala knew. We were going there for a whole week, a whole week in the far flung reaches of the other side of the known world. My mate Peter reckoned that, since we were going somewhere so foreign, it must be in Africa; a place where there would certainly be wildebeest and other strange creatures to deal with! Perhaps also there would be a kraal with pick or ninnies, and men with assegises or assegeese – whatever more than one assegi is. Also he reckoned there would be bare chested ladies there, like there were in the National Geographic Magazine.

Nowadays, much older, and perhaps a little wiser, I know that Chorley (Africa) is as full of bare chested ladies as it is of Eskimos with sunstroke. I also now know that is it a mere thirty minute car journey from where I was born. In those days though it seemed to that nine year old innocent child as though he had left civilisation behind and had indeed entered the heart of darkness.

We took the train from Victoria Station Manchester to Chorley (Africa): twenty odd cubs, Akala and a helper or three, together with a mountain of tents, cooking pots, flour for smoke pasties, and some wildebeest recognition charts. We didn't need any bare chested lady recognition charts – me and Pete knew what they looked like, and had promised to tell the rest of the lads as soon as any happened along. My mother waved me off, tears flowing down her cheeks. I now believe in all sincerity that they were tears of laughter, and were mostly to do with the kit bag.

Let me explain. My mother was a genius and could do almost anything with her hands but making a rucksack with its frame, buckles, leather padding, etc. like what all the other lads had was, I am afraid, beyond her. But, the list of things they had sent me home with did say 'all to be packed in a rucksack or kit bag' though, so mother set out to make me one. If the Paras had been given my mother's home-made kit bags to carry their stuff in when they were yomping across the bogs towards Stanley, we would nowadays, I honesty believe, all be speaking Argentinian and eating Corn Beef Tikka Marsala.

May, 2001

Son of Dib Dib Dib

Baden Powell wrote in *Scouting For Boys,* 'a scout smiles and whistles under all difficulties.' Well short of a direct hit from a neutron bomb I can think of no worse difficulty for a nine years old, undersized, Mancunian cub than a home-made kit bag, longer, thicker and certainly heavier than himself. My mother must have imagined that we had native bearers carrying our stuff on their heads; she certainly can't ever have imagined that I would have to walk the miles from the bus stop to the campsite carrying the kit bag she had made – if she had known then I'm certain she would have come and carried it for me herself. Kit bags are made for sailors and soldiers to carry up gangplanks of troopships on news reels of World War Two – they are not made for small Manchester cubs to have to carry long country miles.

We arrived at Chorley (Africa) station and set off for our camp: twenty odd cubs, Akala and some big scouts who were there to help. All the other cubs had rucksacks, only I had a kit bag. For a hundred yards or so I carried it sailor fashion over my shoulder. Without warning it suddenly slid to the ground. I stood it on end, and with a sudden burst of strength slung it smartly over my shoulder. But I had given it too much wallop, and it threw me on my back on the ground. Winded and unhappy I smiled and whistled as per *Scouting For Boys*, then kicked the kitbag, cursed the kitbag and wrestled with it for a while on the pavement. With the help of a nearby wall I got it back on my shoulder, and set off again whistling and smiling like a madman. Old ladies crossed the road to avoid the deranged grinning midget that was staggering towards them whistling and grinning and carrying a giant, khaki slug.

After another fifty yards my knees began to buckle and I sunk lower and lower, staggering under the weight of this useless lump of a bag. Yet, like the good cub scout I was, I still smiled and whistled as I staggered onwards, my face in a rictus, sinking and sinking, until eventually I looked like a young Toulouse Lautrec with a giant turd on his shoulder. I dropped the kit bag on the deck and stood to straighten my twisted spine and rickety legs. It was a hot summer's afternoon, and I was the very last of a long line of sweating cubs who were all singing the Gin Gan Gooly song as they followed the wobbly bottom of Akala towards our camp.

Two of the big scouts had hung back to pick up any stragglers like myself and to smoke a few sly Players Weights.

'Having trouble kid?' they asked.

'No,' I said, smiling and whistling like a maniac, 'just resting.'

I picked the lifeless and useless khaki sausage up in my arms, and stumbled on for another hundred yards looking as though I was trying to toss a very thick and very floppy caber. Then I fell down.

'We'll give you a hand with it – but it'll cost yer.'

I am still paying off the debt incurred on that hot Lancashire afternoon. Five shillings might not sound much but, with the state of world banking, like one of the poorer African countries, I still owe something like half a million pounds to those two crooks.

At the campsite I kicked the kitbag into a stupor and climbed inside the tent which was already erected, the rest of the pack having been in camp for an hour. I laid out my sleeping bag and my kit. My mother had packed not only enough clothes for a month, my teddy bear and my catechism, but a hot water bottle as well – which did not go down with the rest of the cubs in my tent who were prime candidates for the SAS.

First stop was the country pub in the grounds of which we were camping. There we spent a fortune on bottles of pop which we spent the rest of the day pouring down our necks. The pub was a converted country house, which had been built in the grounds of a monastery destroyed by Henry the Eighth. As the day began to fade into evening and we sat around the campfire eating our smoke pasties, one of the big scouts told us that the grounds of the pub were haunted by a White Friar who had been killed by the

Protestants. His ghost had been seen by loads of people coming out of the lake where they had drowned him. We were camping beside the lake. We were very scared.

Full of pop we crawled into our sleeping bags, and at 'lights out' we were all expected to fall immediately to sleep. Of course none of us did, and for a good hour there was fitful whispering in most of the tents, and much of it was to do with ghostly White Friars.

I had drunk several large bottles of Sarsperella and Dandelion and Burdock, and though my bladder was young and strong and healthy, it was not without its limitations, and in the middle of the night I woke up badly needing a pee. I crossed my legs, thought of sandy deserts, and bit on the sleeping bag – it was no good I had to go. Treading over sleeping, muttering, complaining cubs I stumbled and fumbled my way to the tent flap, and unzipped my way into the cold night air.

It was dark, very dark. A mist had risen from the lake and had covered the campsite turning it into a Hammer Film Set. I walked to the waters edge and started to pee. I wanted to get back in the tent but the peeing wouldn't stop. On and on it went, arcing out into the water, steam rising from the pee to mingle with the fog.

Suddenly a white clad figure, massive, mysterious and ghostly rose up out of the mist close by. I screamed and screamed, shouting that the ghost of the White Friar was coming!! There was the noise of zips and tent flaps being opened, and torches flashed across the dark and mist as the entire camp woke up, and scouts and cubs came running towards me to save me from the ghost of the White Friar – which, it soon became apparent, was actually Akala who had gone out for a pee at the same time as me, and had risen out of the mist from a lady-peeing position like a manifesting monk. I was on potato peeling and smoke pasty making jankers for the rest of the week.

June, 2001

Son of Dib Dib Dib Rides Again

In amongst the stuff in the kit bag my mother had packed for the week's camp was my teddy bear, my hot water bottle, twelve shirts, two sweaters, my catechism, a holy picture of St Jude, the Patron Saint Of Lost Causes, two dozen pairs of socks and a plastic bottle of Lourdes water in the shape of the Virgin Mary, her crown being the stopper. (This last piece of kit was in case of snake bites.) All that, but no underpants – in spite of the fact that I had carried half a ton of gear in a canvas slug half way across Chorley (Africa) – no underpants. Anybody who has read *Scouting For Boys* will know that, as well as teaching you how to recognise wildebeest poo and make yourself a nourishing meal that will sustain you for a thirty day march from nothing but flour and cold water, it also tells you how to deal with laundry while on a trek in the bush – as we were in Chorley, (Africa). If you can't wash your underwear it advises you to beat it soundly with a stick. After five days in the same underpants I took them off and hit them with a stick and they hit me back.

Towards the end of our sojourn in Chorley, (Africa) our Akala announced that we were going on a long walk, but that we were not to worry; dinner would be taken care of by a devilish piece of White Man's Magic called a Biscuit Tin Oven. Biscuit tins in those days, dear reader, were tin boxes, about fourteen inches all round, in which packets of biscuits were displayed in corner shops that smelt of soap, firelighters, mint humbugs and freshly baked bread. The idea of the Biscuit Tin Oven is basically this: you light a big fire then let it die down to glowing embers. In the embers you place the biscuit tin containing, one huge joint of beef, a little salt, and a little water, having remembered first to take all the biscuits out. (*See Crown Court records May 1953 in case of Cubs Various*

– versus Scout Movement National, following Neck End Of Lamb and Jammy Dodger Food Poisoning Incident, Hardcastle Crags 1952). Cover the tin entirely with glowing embers then cover with green leaves and a light scattering of soil. When you return several hours later the meat will be cooked to a turn, it will melt in the mouth, it will be a meal fit for a king, never mind twenty slavering oiks. Twenty slavering oiks prepared the fire, did the business, and left camp on a long hike, trailing behind Akala's pendulous buttocks like a lot of little green jabbering ducks.

There aren't many places you can get lost round Chorley (Africa) but she managed it. Heading for somewhere called Rivington Pike, we ended up staggering through peat bogs and heather clumps on something called Anglezark Moor, and then ended up somewhere else that doesn't have a name at all but is full of swamps and bogholes and rhododendron bushes and midges. And as my mate Pete pointed out, there wasn't a bare chested lady anywhere.

You remember the scene in *The African Queen* where Humphrey Bogart and Katherine Hepburn drag an old boat through leech infested swamps? You remember the scene in *Muppet Platoon,* where Kermit and John Wayne and Sidney Poitier are chained together, and the bloodhounds are after them, and they run splashing through swamps full of snakes and Spanish Moss, and Japanese snipers are shouting things like, 'You can't lun away flom burrits yankee boy!'?

Tish push! I bite my thumb at you! T'were as nothing compared to the sufferings of the St Dunstan The Aggressive, Crumpsall, Manchester, Cub Pack that day in the wilds of Chorley (Africa). We actually lost two kids completely. They were never seen again, vanished, gone, à la *Picnic At Hanging Rock.* Akala told their parents they had run off to join the circus, buying our silence with packets of Rowntree's Fruit Gums.

However, I digress. I have scars on my legs and in my psyche to this day from that slog through the terror filled jungles of wherever we were, and several of the cubs that were with us that day later went on to develop personality disorders and became politicians, lawyers, accountants and the like. Hour after hour we fell and splashed and sweated our way through the swamps of Chorley, (Africa) completely lost. And then my mate Pete, who went on to become a missionary in Real Africa said, 'Please, Akala, the sun's going down. It goes down in the west. We set off this morning walking east. If we follow the sun we might get back.'

We walked towards the glowing orb as it sank in the general direction of Blackpool, and after an hour of more bog and swamp, emerged, scarred, bruised and covered in midge bites not a hundred yards from our camp.

'I told you I'd get you back safely,' said Akala, who had said nothing of the kind – she had in fact been whimpering and snuffling and semi-delirious for the past five hours or so.

Half crazed with hunger we threw the spuds we'd peeled that morning into a dixie, got the fire going again and ran for our knives and forks. When the spuds were ready, Akala scraped the soil back from our old fire, raked away the gunk that had once been leaves, and opened the lid.

Twenty little cubs did Bisto Kid impressions, noses raised to the stars, (it was now night) savouring the aroma. But aroma was all there was. The biscuit tin had turned into a matter transporter. We had been away too long – even for a biscuit tin oven. Akala looked at us guiltily. Inside the tin was a lump of black stuff the size of a dog's nose.

'Well,' she said in a haughty voice, 'you lot are always saying you love Spam fritters anyway.'

We didn't – we hated Spam fritters. We just preferred them to grass and stones.

Terrified, scarified, bruised, eaten by midges, frightened by ghost monks that turn out to be peeing cub-mistresses, fed on Spam fritters, porridge and smoke pasties for a week, and not one tick in my *I Spy Bare Chested Ladies* book. Is it any wonder I deserted?

July, 2001

Things That Go 'Crump' in the Night

The circus animals were nowhere in sight – just one large dollop of elephant doo doo on the hearth rug – so I sought in the foul rag and bone shop of my heart for a theme for the monthly column, sought and sought in vain and was still soughting when suddenly – Shazam! there in the *Guardian* was the headline, *Hikers warned against sitting on time bomb.*

It seems that Dartmoor National Park are just about to issue a leaflet telling walkers how to crap in the wilderness, or to put it more politely, they were about to publish *a lavatorial code of conduct for the moorland* when they had to withdraw it after advice from the MoD. Part of this lavatorial code instructs us to take a small trenching tool with us to dig a hole when we need to defecate on Dartmoor. But the leaflet has had to be put on the back-burner because of all the unexploded bombs lying about around said moor. It appears that the Hound of the Baskervilles would no longer be safe cocking its leg up there.

I reacted to this in two ways. Firstly my comedic mind raced ahead to imagine a scenario where a posse of chums are out on the moor one day. Suddenly one of the posse shouts, 'I say chaps, just dashing off behind the Tor, sudden need to defecate don't you know. Got the old trenching tool as per lavatorial code of conduct, see you in a min.'

The others walk on. A few moments later there is an enormous explosion, and a tattered pair of shorts, followed by an equally tattered pair of boots sail through the air landing some short distance in front of the group.

'I told him that he oughter pack in drinking that real ale,' says his girlfriend picking up the boots. 'These was new and cost ninety five quid; and he's got the car keys! What am I gonner do now?'

The second thought is this:- isn't it time the MoD got out of the National Parks? Dartmoor, the Brecon Beacons and the Northumberland National Park have all been used for live firing exercises as have many other areas of the uplands of these islands. The MoD have also accepted that depleted uranium has been used at some sites, so, if you drop your pants in some of our most beautiful uplands, not only do you face the possibility of a speedy exit from this great stage of fools; if you are lucky enough not to end up sans eyes, sans teeth, sans everything, then you stand a fair chance of being irradiated.

Call me a romantic old fool if you like, but I always imagined the great outdoors as a place of calm and solace, a place where we go to breathe pure air and communicate with whatever god might fill our longings and imaginings. I didn't see it as a place where festering nuclear power stations rot like pustules on the face of the planet, where windfarms flap their questionable grant-supported wings on lovely escarpments, and where instruments of death lie in wait for anybody who follows the lavatorial code of conduct.

The amended code of lavatorial conduct proposed by the MoD recommends that we all defecate SAS style. At first I thought that meant in the Iranian Embassy but it doesn't. It means that you take a sort of poop scoop with you and, *take all your waste matter with you leaving no trace around.*

Now in case you think this column is becoming daily more coprophagic let me point out that I didn't make this stuff up. In fact as a comedian and fantasist of some years standing and falling down, can I respectfully point out that even my fertile imagination wouldn't stretch to creating the kind of nonsense you've been reading above; the sort of stuff the authorities are foisting on us daily.

The great fox hunting debate rages on of course and though I hate to see anything killed for fun, I do feel I ought to point out that there are a lot of other things that need to be sorted out before we take to the streets to protest or otherwise about silly people in red jackets vandalising the countryside. Failing schools and hospital waiting lists are beyond the remit of this column, but when it comes to the Countryside Alliance and their friends the Fuel Tax Protestors blocking the streets of London, I do feel a teeny weeny bit of a right to comment.

I live in a hill farming community, my neighbours are all sheep farmers and most of them work bloody hard to try and wrestle a living from some of the most sour and begrudging land in these islands. At a time of failing markets and uncertainty let us give the farmers grants for the stewardship of the uplands, for walling, for maintaining old barns, for hedging, for not throwing black plastic baling bags and twine in the rivers or down the potholes, for not overgrazing the hills so that the mountains are eaten to the bone, for working with the authorities in maintaining footpaths and access. I know that in some areas these kinds of grants are already available but more needs to be done.

More people go to the Peak District National Park in five years than would ever have gone to the Dome, if they'd kept it open for a trillion years. (And while I'm on about it let me tell you that I refused to go to the Dome – because I thought they should have spent the money on new roofs and inside toilets for schools).

Can you imagine what our National Parks could have done with all the money that was tossed away on the Dome?

There used to be a character in a kids' comic – I think it was the Wizard – who only had one line – *Daft I call it.* Well daft I call it too; and when the Countryside Alliance and their right wing terrorist chums parade through London, let those of us who can stomach going down there, hold up placards saying, *Daft I Call It*; and furthermore, if the Countryside Alliance want something useful to do, why don't they go and borrow some mine detectors from their mates at the MoD and get out there and clear the hills of bombs and depleted uranium so we can all go and have a crap in peace? Or is that too sensible?

April, 2001

The Hills are Not Alive with the Sound of Yodelling Ducks

I must stop reading stuff. It's all starting to have an effect. It's my mother's fault of course, for teaching me to read when I was four; ever since then I've read everything I can get my hands on. I'm one of those hopeless literatureholics, the kind of person who, if there's no *Guardian* or *Independent* at the breakfast table, reads the back of the cereal packet, or the nutritional information printed on the side of a yogurt carton. I get through three or four books a week, and my house is in very serious danger of sinking into the earth from the weight of books on its walls.

It was reading that upset me this week. Not a book, but two pieces of print: one was an email from a mate; the other a slip of a paragraph in the *Guardian*. Both the following facts are true. The email stated quite baldly that it is a scientific truth that the duck is the only creature on the face of the planet whose call doesn't have an echo; while the article in the newspaper was about a magazine called, *The Drunkard*, published in America and aimed at serious professional liver-cripplers. The magazine contains such useful information as, *staggering while drunk uses up more calories than walking soberly.* Just as you hear smokers saying – 'So! If I smoke I'll die early and won't be a drain on the pension services,' – I can imagine heavy drinkers now claiming that their colossal boozing is a way of slimming (and furthermore helps Society in that it means they aren't taking up space on the treadmill at the gym.)

Back to the duck. This crumb of information concerning duck-echolessness lodged itself in my mind and began to irritate it, like a piece of grit under an eyelid. Nights were spent sleeplessly staring at the ceiling while my partner snored softly into her pillow. I pictured ducks waddling into the whispering gallery at St Paul's Cathedral in London and emitting a faint 'quack', only to find their call swallowed up in the gloom. I imagined a posse of mallards on the brink of the Grand Canyon quacking away, their little song fading into nothingness, while beside them a mixed bunch of basset hounds, bantam cocks and kookaburras sent their cries rattling and echoing round the canyon. I imagined Swiss ducks in lederhosen climbing the Altfrau, the Jungfrau and the Muttondressedaslambfrau, and yodelling their hearts out to find that there were no answering echoes. I determined to put this astonishing theory to the test.

If you walk from Selside in Ribblesdale, over by Thieves Moss to Clapham you will find, just beyond the Moss a small natural limestone amphitheatre. If you stand on the footpath there and make a loud noise you will hear up to five perfect echoes, hardly diminishing in strength. Over the years I have variously amazed and bored scores of children by taking them there, telling them to stand still and listen, while emitting one of my taxi-calling, two fingers in mouth, whistles. They have either stared in amazement or yawned with ennui as the echoes went spinning round the limestone walls of the cove.

So I had the place for my experiment; all I needed was a duck. I don't have any ducks myself and the phrase 'Can I borrow your duck?' is not one that trips lightly off the tongue. There's a Chinese restaurant in Settle – perhaps they had some ducks that hadn't been crispy-Pekinged yet? But what would I say when they asked me why I wanted to borrow one? 'I want to take it for a walk up the mountain?' I think not. In any case there's probably a law against it: The Duck And Rambler Act 1947 which makes it an offence to take an unlicensed duck on a public footpath with the intention of forcing it to quack. I suppose I could have bought one of those plastic Acme duck calls you see in gun shops, but I didn't think of it at the time; and I suppose that, for my experiment to be respected in scientific circles, it had to be the real thing.

In the end I stole one, well, borrowed one actually, from off the river at Horton: a public duck; one of those everyday ducks you see, all shiny bottle green bib and orange feet; a quotidian duck. I snuck up on it and shoved it under my oxter when nobody (particularly the duck) was looking.

It wasn't happy. It wanted to be with its fellow mallards mating and bobbing up and down, snuffling about, looking for caddis grubs and whatever other filthy stuff ducks eat; instead it was in my rucksack being taken for a long walk under Ingleborough.

I got to Thieves Moss, took it out and held the duck up facing the limestone crags. It stared silently at the strange, waterless and duckless landscape before it.

I waited. No quack. I made tentative quacking noises myself. Still no quack. I made loud quacking noises. Still nothing from the real duck. I whistled and my whistle bounced and echoed all over the cwm. The duck looked at me and made a faint, grumbling, half-hearted noise that sounded like it might build up to a quack but didn't.

It was at that moment that a posse of drunken ramblers arrived on a walk sponsored by *The Drunkard.* They crested a rise to find a man holding up a duck as though to show it the view. I could see by the way they were staggering that they were obviously using vast amounts of calories, and their tee-shirts carried the legend, 'Barnsley And Wombwell – Boozing, Formation Drinking And Weight Loss Club.'

It took them a while to stagger up to me, and several of them fell down, quite heavily too, but after a few minutes the combined intellectual strength of fourteen or so South Yorkshire drunks was brought to bear on my problem. One of them, with the look of a sage and the breath of a donkey on a fish and old socks diet chuckled and said wisely, 'There's an owd Barnsley proverb tha knows – *Tha can carry a duck up t' mountain but tha can't mek it quack.* Think on owd love.' Then he passed out.

And do you know, he was right – the bloody thing never did quack, so the jury on duck-echoes is still out.

March, 2004

The Wobbleydale Booze Experience

Now I don't want to upset anybody, and I'm sure that there's something really interesting and worthy behind it all, but the other day my flabber was more ghasted than ever before, and all because of a leaflet I picked up in a café in the Dales when I was out walking in Widdledale. You know the kind of thing I mean, an A4 sheet folded in three, nicely printed with a picture on the front; the sort of information sheet local tourist boards encourage, telling you to *Visit Neat Scar Caves*, or *Have A Great Day Out at Saggy Bottom Steam Railway.*

Over the years several Scandinavian forests have been transmogrified into these leaflets as tourism has developed into this Island's only major growth industry. When on tour slogging my way round the theatres and arts centres of this fair land, I have collected these things by the handful, wondering whether my idle moments between shows might be cheered by a visit to *The York Dungeon* or *Barometer World*, or my life transformed by a day out at *Sellafield Visitor Centre* or *The World Of Bakelite.*

The leaflet that I picked up the other day though took several cream crackers, *A Great Day Out For the Family*, it promised, and went on to warn me, *You mustn't miss the Widdledale Cheese Experience!!* Entrance to the Widdledale Cheese Experience is only £2 (Concessions £1.25) and includes a tour of a typical Dales farmhouse kitchen circa 1935, a wander through the cheese museum, a real life cheese-making session with hands-on experience for the children and finally an audio visual presentation, *Cheese Through the Ages.*

I can picture it now: the lights dim in the small theatre, and the screen begins to glow with a picture of a primordial swamp, dinosaurs loom above tangled prehistoric undergrowth as the music of *Thus Spake Zarathustra* fills the room in surround sound, and the slide cross-fades to a picture of Early Cheese Man milking a goat into a stone bucket. Then a deep mid-Atlantic voice intones, 'From the Earliest Times, Cheese has been Man's Best Friend. Nobody knows who invented cheese, but what we do know is that it has been around for a long time.' The slides cross-fade again to shots of Tutenkhamen as the voice drones on over some quasi-Egyptian music, 'The Pharaohs had their favourite cheeses embalmed and placed in their tombs alongside their mummies so that they could journey on with them into the realms of the Dead ...' and so it goes on, and on, and pigging on!

Now I don't particularly object to any of this, (I do, if I'm honest) and I'm not elitist enough to suggest that we should all be walking the hills reciting Li Po and Wordsworth, communing with nature to the exclusion of everything and everyone else, but it does seem to me that this country we spend our leisure hours walking through is swiftly becoming a giant theme park. There seems to be hardly a puddle more than seven feet across that isn't advertised as a Trout Farm, *Come And Feed The Fish!!* the sign invites us, and we do, and we pay for the pigging privilege. *Visit the Grotshire Heritage Centre,* we are told and we do, to look at ploughs and butter churns, and rusty, eye watering things that were once used for turning bulls into bullesses.

I know that I have made passing references to this in previous articles, but at the risk of becoming boring, where is all this going to end up? As everything becomes a commodity and an *experience*, is Englandland PLC (not forgetting its sister companies Scotlandland PLC, and Walesland PLC) going to employ us all as extras in this great drama? And if the landscape we walk through and climb in also becomes an *experience*, then how long is it before there is pressure on to build a railway to the top of the Ben or Scafell?

The concept of landscape as commodity isn't one we should be laughing at, because somebody, somewhere, I assure you, is taking it very seriously indeed; and just as we no longer have any real right to roam in this island other than on authorised paths or permitted open country, it is possible that water and forestry boards as well as private landowners will start to see the moors and mountains as leisure activity areas (over and above the hunting and shooting) and will not only try and find ways of charging walkers and climbers for their sport, but may also open the land out to other, less eco-friendly pursuits.

We already have a problem with off road vehicles and trail riders churning up bridleways, and destroying the quiet and solitude of the hills, and in at least one place in the Dales there is a company advertising, *Off-road Safaris* with chains of up to half a dozen Range Rovers carrying tourists along a mediaeval monk's lane and over pristine moorland in a *real wilderness experience.*

I hate to sound like a prophet of doom and I'm sure some of you will be thinking, 'He's off his chump – never in a month of Sundays' – but who would have thought fifteen years ago that trespass would have been made a criminal offence or that the water boards and their great gathering grounds would be privatised? If the Kinder Mass Trespass took place today they wouldn't be sending six ramblers to prison for 'riotous assembly', they'd be sending all four hundred and odd of them to Strangeways for Criminal Trespass. There's an old Chinese curse, *May you live in interesting times.* It's a subtle wily oriental curse but I think I know what it means. Interesting times are when all the excrement gets introduced to the air-conditioning.

As people get more leisure time and remote areas become more accessible then there will be increased pressure for commercialisation. How long before there's an IMAX at Culloden and a *Massacre Experience* at Glencoe (*Total Realistic Re-enactment* of the butchering complete with son-et-lumiere). The Romans gave the Proles bread and circuses to keep them down. We get off-road safaris and the Widdledale Cheese Experience. We live in interesting times.

June, 1996

Winston Churchill and the Sticky Bomb

As Dr. Johnston once said to Boswell, as they were rummaging through the ashtrays of the Clachaig Inn looking for a few tabs they could cannibalise for a rollie, 'Tha knaws Bozzers, the problem with bed and breakfast joints is that you have to share them with all kind of kith, kin and assorted mankind – and stap my vitalls but what a rum lot some of them kith and kin can be!'

Rum is not the word. I was once walking in the Welsh borders, and stopped the night at a small B&B. It was clean and welcoming, smelt of home cooking, had fat armchairs and enough Readers Digest Condensed Books to keep you occupied for a couple of years; and, if you didn't like Neville Chute and Nancy Mitford, you could always opt for bound copies of *The Radnorshire Bloodstock Journal 1938-1942*, or *Lives Of The Great Methodist Preachers* – all ten volumes of it.

However, I digress. The day had been wet and glum, and a walk along the old drove roads had drenched us to the skin so, after a shower and a change of clothes we worked our way through a fine dinner. Afterwards we sat in the residents' lounge debating on whether to go to the pub or go to the pub, and had just decided to go to the pub when the door opened and what I can only describe as a man entered.

Those of you who have read Coleridge's poem *The Ancient Mariner* may remember that, once the wedding guest is transfixed by the grey beard loon with the glittering eye, he has to listen to the entire story top to bottom. So it was with the greybeard loon that had just come in and was now leaning against the sideboard with its pot Alsatian dog, its pot spaniel and its pot little girl holding up her skirts to dance.

'I'd have been a millionaire now if it weren't for Churchill,' he spouted into an otherwise silent room.

As opening remarks go, that one was fairly interesting and had me wondering whether he'd lost his millions in a hand of three card brag to that cigar smoking cherubic old war dog. We adopted the, 'embarrassed English person position' and, instead of getting up and manhandling him roughly through the front door, we pretended to be engrossed in our books: *Welsh Spoon Designers of the Eighteenth Century*, and *Diseases Of Poultry, Some Answers.*

'The robbing bastard. No wonder he could afford cigars.' was the second episode in what we now understood was to be an epic.

'He's not here,' I said hoping to divert him.

'Who?' he asked.

'Churchill. He's not here, he's staying at the Glyndower Arms up the road.'

'He's dead,' the grey beard loon replied, obviously not one to be diverted.

'Oh that Churchill: Sunday painter, made walls, bombed Dresden and all that.'

'The very one. He robbed me of my rightful fortune.'

'How was that then?' my companion asked cutting to the quick, obviously wanting to get back to his book and find out what to do if one of his Rhode Island Leghorns ever got beak warble fly, wing alopecia, or wattle droop.

'Sticky bomb,' was the answer.

'Sticky bomb!?' was also the question.

'I'm the man who invented the sticky bomb.'

Suddenly the pub was starting to seem a long long way away.

In situations like this I've been known to feign a fainting fit, or to invent a long lost companion that I've suddenly spotted across a crowded room; but we were trapped and, worse still, my companion had decided that the man was worth talking to.

'How was that then?'

'It was in the war, and I was playing with my little boy. He had a toy tank and some soldiers, and – well you know what little boys are like – he suddenly produced a giant bogey from his nose and tried to flick it off. It got stuck to the toy tank and he tried to shake it off. But it wouldn't shake off. And suddenly it struck me!'

'Another bogey?'

'No – I had a thought. *What about if bombs stuck to tanks like that? What about if I could make a grenade that would stick to the wall of a tank?'*

I looked to see if the window was open, but it had been painted shut in the thirties. There was no escape, and my friend was hooked now like a trout on a fat worm in a flood.

'So what did you do?' There was no trace of sarcasm in the question my friend asked. I, on the other, hand had conjured up in my mind the vision of millions of civilians collecting nasal membrane detritus for the war effort along with aluminium pans and iron railings. Posters proclaiming, 'Bogies Against Hitler!' would have adorned the walls of rural post offices; schoolchildren would have been given prizes for the biggest snot collection. Pathé Newsreels would have showed plucky English villages cheering off their bogey collection as it rattled out of the village on the backs of lorries driven by cheery British Tommies smoking Woodbines. But I said nothing.

'I got a stick and a tin grenade, and covered it with the kind of glue they put on flypaper and threw it at the side of my car.'

'Did it work?'

'Not at first. It took me a lot of goes before I got the mixture right.'

'By which time your car was covered in dead flies?' I offered.

'We were at war!' he glared back at me. 'We all had to make sacrifices. Any road up; eventually I got the mix right and sent all my research papers to Churchill at the war office. He wrote back and said they were interesting but that he didn't think my ideas were of any use. Then before I knew it they were all over the place.'

'Sticky bombs?'

He nodded, 'Stopped a lot of tanks did my sticky bombs. And I never made a penny out of it.'

'Do you not think somebody else at the MoD might have come

up with the idea?' I suggested, remembering how in the late seventies I had invented the CD while drunk in Inverness, only to find that Philips the electronics giant had the same idea.

'No. It was my idea they took. You couldn't get a roll of flypaper for the rest of the war. Churchill robbed me of my patent. I would have been worth millions. Won the war did my sticky bombs, but I never made a penny out of it.'

'You invent anything else?'

'Plastic dog poop.'

'What were you going to do with that?'

'Drop it in front of the Germans. Very particular about their boots, the Jerries. Slow down their advance.'

'Wouldn't they suss that they were false?'

'One in twenty would be real. Jerry could never have relaxed. I sent one to Stalin. Could have saved Leningrad my plastic dog doo.'

The woman of the house called him from the kitchen. He made a move, we saw light between him and the door and fled to the pub.

There was nobody there all that long night but us and the landlord. Remind me to tell you some time how he invented underground aeroplanes and dehydrated water.

August, 2001

Fixing Broken Chickens in the Hindu Kush

A lot of people think us writers have an easy doo of it, viz all we have to do is scribble our stuff and the publisher, breathless with excitement and gratitude, tears the work of genius out of our hands and rushes round the corner to the printers; following which two weeks later it comes out to ruptured applause from Al and his pal Sundry. Wrong. I've got two novels, a book of poetry and a book of short stories languishing in the cupboard that nobody seems to want, and I could paper the walls of several large houses with the rejection slips. And, even though I've had four travel books published, the new one seems to be to publishing what Herod is to Mothercare. It's called *Fixing Broken Chickens In The Hindu Kush* – and, should you wonder at the title gentle reader – here's the reason why.

It was an early summer afternoon in the Yorkshire Dales, way back in the Mists of Time a few years back, a day of great beauty, the air calm, the sun shining on the valley. A pair of buzzards were circling over Helm Knott, and the back lawn of my house in Dentdale was so covered in gear that it looked like an accident in an outdoors shop. Spread out on the grass were: tent, sleeping bag, cagoule, carabineers, rope; prussic loops, ice axe, crampons, wash bag, clothes, medicines, snow-goggles, sun creams, my copy of Joyce's *Ulysses* that had already been to the Himalayas four times and was looking dog and cat-eared now; three waterproof journals made in Edinburgh, the last of the bunch – now that the firm that made them has closed, a fountain pen and loads of cartridges, my cameras and lenses and film enough for a three month trip, my compass and maps and my passport with the all important visas for Pakistan, India and Nepal.

The camera stuff was going in a Pelican case while the crampons and ice axe were going in a big blue polythene expedition drum together with two bottles of Bushmills Whisky, for medicinal purposes; everything else was going in my kit bag, a huge shapeless yellow thing that packed easily but had the native porters and ponymen grumbling all the time because it was such a clumsy load. It wasn't that it was big: like me it was the wrong shape: short and squat and with a mind of its own. I had watched porters wrestle with it, kick it, maul it, lash it with rope and assume positions on it that I'd only seen before in the Kama Sutra, and still the damn thing lay squat and ugly on their backs like a big yellow snail's house. Each night I would open the kit bag to find my clothes in a mess, *Ulysses* bent double and the toothpaste all over my wash bag. But, in terms of volume and toughness, it was the best kit bag I'd ever had, and it suited me.

I slung the stuff in and sat on the bench in the afternoon sun watching the school bus crawling along the valley below on its way to pick the kids up. It's always strange sitting like this before a major trip in the mountains: looking down at the valley, wondering what the Hell I'm doing leaving a place as beautiful as this: then I remember the wonderful times I've had in the Himalayas, and the new places I'm heading for, and I start to get excited again, like a kid on the last day of school who knows that the long summer holidays are stretching out before him.

Then something brought my thoughts back to the first time I walked in India and how, in many of the villages we'd passed through, there had been people asking for medicine. In some simple cases I'd been able to help: Rinstead pastilles at the Muni Gompa had cleared up a monk's mouth ulcer in a couple of days; a bit of iodine and cleanliness had cleaned up an ulcerated heel in one Zanskar village. I won't dish out antibiotics, and wherever possible I get the people to go to their local clinics or use whatever herbal medicine they've been used to – there's nothing worse than 'sahibs' who think they can cure the ills of the developing world with a paracetamol and a bit of White Man's Magic.

But one thing had disturbed me in particular. In many of the villages along the trail I'd seen horrific gashes and wounds, some caused by falls, some by knives or scythes that had been swung too clumsily. I'd never been able to help in those cases: butterfly strips can't pull together a really deep gash. My daughter Emma is a doctor with a good few years experience in trauma medicine; she was home living with us at the time so I asked her if she'd show me how to stitch up a wound.

'You mean suture,' she said.

'Suture self,' I quiped badly. She didn't even smile. 'Well, stitches, sutures, whatever you call them.'

'Get some boneless chicken breasts, and we can practice on them. That's how we did it in medical school.'

That evening, back from Sainsbury's with a dozen chicken breasts, and watched by Reuben and Huxley, our two black and white cats, we attacked the chicken breasts with kitchen knives until they were all deeply scarred and I watched as she stitched one back together on the garden table. After a couple of goes I managed to do a reasonable job of one or two myself; nothing that a plastic surgeon would have been proud of, but in the high mountains of Zanskar and Ladakh or in one of the villages of Baltistan, nobody's going to worry too much if the stitches aren't all Saville Row and Harley Street.

'Well,' I said as we took the stitches out and put the chicken bits in a tikka mix to marinade, 'I've added another arrow to the quiver: While I'm in the Hindu Kush I can fix any broken chickens I come across.'

January, 2005

Moscow Riley's Crutches

It struck me the other day that, compared to the writings of Bill Bryson and Wilfrid Thesiger, much of what I write is, as Guiseppe Verdi once said, *La Triviata* – but then again I'm not on the money Bryson and Thesiger get. If you pay ant doo doo you get aardvarks – that's my philosophy. So though my meanderings may not be world class, they may suit the man or woman who gets on the Clapham Omnibus to go and buy a pair of Brasher Boots, and it is to him or her that I direct this little bit of nonsense.

It's all to do with why we go out into the Great Outdoors.

Some of us do it because of a spirit of adventure, to push ourselves to the limit. Some of us do it to commune with the spirit of the earth, to lose ourselves amongst the great open spaces of God's breath. Others, like the late Alfred Wainwright, do it to get away from the wife.

I do it for some of the above, but also for the stories. You see I believe that wherever we walk, unless we are pushing unknown routes in previously un-trod places, we are walking on the stories of the past.

If you follow the old green lane from Bainbridge to Cam Fell in the Yorkshire Dales, you walk on a road that the Romans made; and that itself lies on a track tramped into the fells by the feet of Bronze Age tribes that wandered those hills. If you walk the coastal path of Devon and Cornwall, you drop from cliff top to beach and back again, following the old ways of the smugglers, and the coastguards who were out to catch them; and if you go to County Clare, Ireland and walk the Cliffs of Moher up to St. Brigid's Well, you will go the way of Moscow Riley and his crutches.

Did I tell you the story of Moscow Riley and his Crutches? No?

Well settle down and I will begin.

Moscow wasn't his real name of course. Moscow worked on the West Clare Railway during the nineteen thirties and, unusually for the time, was in the union. In those days, when Ireland was run by the Roman Catholic Taliban, to be in the union marked you down as a Trotskyite atheist communist.

One day Moscow Riley was uncoupling some goods wagons in the sidings when suddenly he found himself caught between two wagons whose brakes had failed. Crushed by the buffers he dropped between the wheels stunned. When they pulled him out again it seemed that his back was broken, and that he was paralysed from the waist down.

At Tralee Hospital teams of doctors examined him and X-rayed him all to no purpose. Though he seemed only to be bruised and shaken, Moscow Riley appeared to be paralysed from the waist down and could no longer walk.

The compensation hearing was long and costly, and the railway company's lawyers and the insurance company's medical experts did all they could to prove that Moscow was shamming. In the end though, the judge gave Moscow the benefit of the doubt and awarded him a massive fifty thousand pounds compensation, which is probably equivalent to eleven zillion pounds in today's money.

On the steps of the court the reporters besieged Moscow as he stood there on his crutches looking the future in the eye, and they asked him what he was going to do with the money.

'I'm going to take a taxi to St. Brigid's Well,' he told them.

Now St. Brigid's Well is one of the holiest wells in the whole of that Holy land of Ireland. Pure water bubbles out of the earth at the end of a short tunnel, and the walls of that tunnel are draped and festooned with bandages and old medicine bottles and the photographs of people who have come here, drunk the water, and been cured. Moscow Riley arrived that miraculous day with the reporters in train, made his way on crutches to the back of the tunnel and took a long, slow drink from the holy well. Before the eyes of the multitude the strength and feeling came back into his legs and trunk, and with a cry of, 'Praise God, His Holy Virgin Mother and St. Brigid I'm cured!' Moscow Riley flung away his crutches and leaped and jumped about like a gosoon.

The insurance company and the railway company and all their medical experts frothed and foamed at the mouth, and the chairman of the board had a minor heart attack, but this was Catholic Ireland in the nineteen thirties, and who was going to say that a miracle had not occurred? Who in the whole of County Clare was going to say that God did not move in mysterious ways, and that, furthermore, He had every right to cure whoever He wanted – whether he was the communist Moscow Riley or the Reverend Bishop of Cork. And if you go to St. Brigid's Well today, in that little spot just above the Cliffs of Moher with their seven hundred feet of sheer rock falling to the rolling Atlantic waves below, you will see Moscow Riley's crutches hanging there above the bandages and the pill boxes and the pictures of the Sacred Heart.

Now, to go off at several tanents, a couple of days ago I bumped into a pal of mine Dimitri who runs a Greek restaurant down the bottom end of Deansgate, Manchester.

'Fancy climbing Mount Olympus?' he asked.

'Yes,' I said.

Olympus, as you probably know, was the abode of the gods (Zeus in particular) who have been sat up there for aeons eating ambrosia (though what gods were doing eating tinned rice pudding is beyond me).

Any road up, as you read this, dear man or woman on the Clapham omnibus, I will be slogging my way up Mount Olympus with a Manchester Greek friend who was once in a band called Alberto y Los Trios Paranoias and you can't get much weirder than that.

Perhaps we'll meet Moscow Riley on the top eating rice pudding with Zeus – you never know.

June, 2000

Zen and the Art of Kissing Dead Saints' Feet

The old proverb, *When in Rome do what the Romans do*, is one of those sayings like, *It's a long road that has no turnings*, and *Life's too short to dance with ugly women* that has its uses but can also get you into some trouble. Having been schooled in the Crumpsall College of Aphorism Adages Axioms and Mottoes I take such saws and dictums with a bucket of salt.

Dancing with an incredibly ugly, but rich woman, for example, can lengthen your life considerably if you are a very handsome young man on the verge of starvation. On the other hand the M1 – which has no turnings at all – is a very long road indeed, so the above saying is in fact redundant in today's world, when reeling English drunks no longer make the rolling English roads. As for the Rome thingy – well I was reminded of that old saw as I sat down to write this piece all about how to behave when on the trek in foreign parts.

I don't mean something as simple as telling any southerners that are reading this that, when they are rambling in northern climes and are offered a cup of tea which is too hot they should waft it with their flat hats. I mean more important things such as native dances and native booze. After years of travel and dozens of expeditions in all kinds of strange corners of the world like Zanskar and Ladakh, the Hindu Kush and Luddenden Foot, I feel I have some experience in coping with local conditions, and can offer a little timely advice to all would be travellers. I offer the following in the spirit of fellow travelling at no charge.

To begin at the beginning: The flight.

Don't drink when flying. If you are the pilot you need all your wits about you in case you fly into a mountain because some mountains are very hard. If you are a passenger and drink a lot it won't matter as much, since you don't have all those dials and sticks and pedals to worry about. However there are drawbacks. Not only does booze de-hydrate you, but like an airborne Jekyll and Hyde, you will find that you have become a pain in the bum to the other passengers. If you become a very big pain in the bum you may also find that you have been put off the plane in Burma where some small but powerful policemen will be waiting to liven up the soles of your feet with rattan canes.

Once you get to your destination observe the local dress. If you are a woman this can save you from a lot of harassment. Walking around in shorts that show the cheeks you don't put blusher on might be fine in Ibiza; in Yemen or Saudi Arabia, on the other hand, you may well find yourself as part of the Friday evening beheading, truncating and burning through the gristle of the nose show. It's no use complaining that such countries are backward; they aren't interested in your opinions, and if you want to go there abide by their laws. After all you would presumably object to a South Sea Islander stood at the frozen pizza counter in Sainsbury's clothed in nothing but a wide smile, a dried snake headband and a penis gourd.

There was only one time when not observing the local dress code saved me from getting into trouble. I was rambling along through the mountains on one of the Greek Islands one fine day with my wife, Pat, and Emma, one of my daughters. The day was hot and sunny, bees hummed in the wild mountain thyme, and goats, with no thought of the skewers and charcoal that lay ahead of them, baaed and maaed and tinkled their bells in the scrub and the rocky gullies.

As we trundled along we came upon a long procession of bearded priests and altar boys leading a crowd of local villagers all dressed in the local costume (sort of black with a touch of black). They were heading for a large monastery on the top of the hill, and being nosy we followed. When we got to the monastery, Pat and Emma, who were dressed in skirts and blouses and were wearing head scarves were invited in to the ceremony. I was wearing the

Pom's foreign travel uniform: shorts and a singlet, a beanie hat and a peeling nose. I rightly thought it disrespectful to go inside the church, so I sat in the monastery garden watching the sunlight on the mountains and listening to the tinkling of goat bells and the bleating of the goats as the flocks made their way down the mountainside. At one time I must have snoozed off because I woke up to find Pat and Emma sitting beside me an hour or so later gagging and pale.

It seemed that, once a year on this island, the dehydrated corpse of Saint Dolmades Tzatsiki is pulled out of his glass coffin, and the richly bejeweled cadaver is laid out for the faithful to see. Not just to see but to kiss.

Understandably this is seen as a very great occasion and a very great honour. For some reason the big toe of the right foot was the chosen spot, and Pat and Emma, who had been suitably dressed, had the very great honour of pressing their lips on the big toe of the left foot of a very well dressed, but very dead and smelly saint.

We went straight to the nearest taverna where they washed away the smell of the incense and the taste of dead saint with several glasses of retsina and ouzo, and went down the mountain as though they had just been presented with their legs and were learning how to use them.

Now, from appropriate dress to the Englishman's nemesis: foreign languages. I cringe every time I hear some Brit in a foreign clime think that all they have to do is speak English slowly and loudly and everyone will understand them. If that doesn't work they shout, 'You don't speak a da English?' and, as the poor local stares at them in bafflement, they yell, 'Well fetch me somebody who does!'

Ah the days when every pickaninny knew their place, and God was an Englishman.

You and I, of course, are different. So – always try the language wherever you are. Even if you only manage to master a few words it shows some respect of the local culture and can also result in some delightful misunderstandings. My *Get By In Urdu* book has been a great help in my travels in Pakistan and also means that I can show off in curry houses in Bradford and Manchester. Unfortunately once I've got past page four and *tatti kahan hai*? (Where is the toilet?) I'm back to ordering by numbers. (By the way, since Hindi and Urdu are virtually the same languages you get two prizes with one ball). The same is not true for Dutch which my Yorkshire pal, Spike, who comes from Cleckhuddersfax, speaks fluently. With Dutch all you get is Dutch. And since the language sounds like somebody constantly trying to cough up a fly while singing the Sex Pistols greatest hits, and since there aren't any mountains there, it's highly unlikely that us outdoor lot will ever have to learn it.

I was in Rawalpindi once, wandering round the Rajah Bazaar, one of the biggest street markets in Pakistan. I was fairly conspicuous with my cameras and tape recorder, photographing and recording the sights and sounds of the market, and I suddenly noticed a young man standing by one of the stalls staring at me.

'Asalaam aleikum.' *God be with you*, I said.

'Waileikum asalaam.' *And with you also*, he answered.

'Apkaa kya hal he?' *How are you?* I asked

'Me thik hun.' *I'm fine*, he answered.

He stared at me more intently.

'Apkaa nam kya he?' *What is your name?* he asked.

'Mira nam Mike he.' *My name is Mike,* I answered.

'I thought it was you. I used to watch you on telly when I were a kid,' he said in a heavy Bradford accent.

It turned out he was in Rawalpindi visiting his grandparents, and that his brother runs a fruit stall on Skipton Market. So you see, if I hadn't had those few words of Urdu I would never have been able to get my bananas at half price. So think on, and get them phrases learned.

April, 2000

Zen and the Art of Eating Used Babies Nappies

As part two of my *Helpful Handy Hints for Innocent Trekkers and Travellers*, I would like to deal with local food and customs. When it comes to food, trekkers and travellers often find that they are faced with a strange dilemma: what do you do? Do you choose to die of starvation, or do you die of eating what your host has just put before you; which looks like crocodile afterbirth smothered in the sludge that they dredge out of the bottom of a park rowing boat at the end of the summer, all lightly tossed with dead maggot puree on a bed of crisp banana leaves? More importantly will they be offended if you don't eat it? And are these people the kind of people who, by tradition, simply have to kill you if you offend them?

My answer to this is: always take a good look at the locals. Are they dead? No, and they eat crocodile afterbirth and rowing boat sludge on banana leaves all the time. QED unless you really fancy trying to finish the trek on a diet of water and sand, you'd better tuck in, and last one to the umbilical cord is a sissy.

In the Himalayas the food, while basic, is often terrific: lots of good currys and fresh chapatis. In Africa the food can be a bit dodgy (I once ate a dish of things with too many legs covered in peas accompanied by a drink made from roots bashed in a hollow log – I was drunk and ill for a week) but, having said that, the best food I ever had on a trek was on Kilimanjaro – all the vegetables were fresh and organic, grown on nowt but muck and the taste exploded in your mouth as you suddenly remembered what tomatoes used to taste like.

It is in America, where they have perfected the art of growing tomatoes the size of your head that taste of nothing, where I had one of my worst food experiences ever. While walking along the

Appalachian trail I stopped off for a few days with a couple of poet friends who live near Highlands, North Carolina. While there we were invited round to the house of another couple for supper one night. I'm afraid I supped 'not wisely but too well' on some moonshine whisky that the host had got from an 'old timer up in the holler,' and so I ate the food put before me, (which seemed to be a bowl of very ordinary looking chilli) without any comment. It tasted good, very good, with lots of chilli and what seemed to be lumps of tuna or swordfish or something. A Jewish lady literary agent from New York who happened to be also staying with the poets, and who also happened to be slightly deaf, was sat beside me at the table.

'What's the meat?' she asked me. 'It's delicious.'

'Don't know,' I mumbled in Crumpsaldrunkenese, 'I'll find out. Excuse me Bro. What's in the chilli?'

The answer was short but clear. 'Rattler. Killed it myself this morning. Big mother long as my arm.'

'What did he say?'

I am no expert on Jewish dietary laws but I do know that Jews do not eat shellfish, pigs, or anything that crawls on its belly (so presumably if there was such a thing as Jewish cannibals they wouldn't eat politicians). I told the lady that it was rattlesnake and she was noisily sick in the hosts' gun cabinet.

The worst food I have ever had though, ever, at any time, anywhere in the Cosmos, the universe, our house, anywhere at all, was in Iceland. Now Iceland is a beautiful country; the landscape is great, the walking is terrific, the people are wonderful (even if there are only two names in the whole country and everybody is called either Eva Gudmundersonsdatter or Gudmunder Evasdatterson). And what can I say about a place that sells more books per capita than any in the world, that has poetry on TV every night after the news, and where everybody has a hot pot in their garden? This hot pot by the way is not a Lancashire stew but a sort of open air jacuzzi, so that you can get drunk, run across the snow and sit in the hot pot with your bum poaching while icicles form on your hair, eyebrows and anything else you've been stupid enough to leave out.

However I digress. It was there in that land of volcanoes, high culture and parboiled blonde, teenage girls that I had my culinary cumuppance. I had been walking from somewhere called Porksmork to somewhere else called Morkspork, and had returned to the city after days in the volcanic ash fields lying on permafrost looking up at the Northern Lights. Back in Reykjavik some very kind Icelandic friends took me out for a meal and treated me to a very expensive Icelandic delicacy, *Thorksmorkshtinkenlangentime fishenfestern* – long dead shark that has been buried in the sand on the beach until it has rotted, at which point it is dug up again and served only in expensive restaurants in OXO cube sized portions stuck on tooth picks at ten quid a shot.

It reminded me of a baby's nappy, and I don't mean a fresh one. I mean a nappy that has been on a teething baby all night, and it's nine o'clock, and you've overslept, and it's standing in the cot banging things, and wants feeding and wants this disgusting, festering mess taking off its little botty right now. I don't make a habit of eating baby's soiled nappies, and to be honest I don't suppose you do either gentle reader. There may be some of you out there who dress up in women's clothing (particularly if you are a woman) and there may even be some of you out there who climb Snowdon while whistling the hits of Barry Manilow, but I doubt if there are many of you out there who would eat a soiled baby's nappy. That dear reader is what I ate; after a week of wandering round ash cones and lava fields and glaciers, after days of crossing swollen rivers and boiling mud fields, that is what my hosts offered me: baby's nappy on a stick.

And why didn't I refuse it? Have you read the Icelandic saga of Eric the Ever So Easily Slighted? That's the one where Eric slices of the head of the bloke who leaves a bit of pie crust on his plate. I ate that baby's nappy, and I smiled all the way through it. Then I got very very drunk indeed.

May, 2000

Zen and the Art of Shouting at Blisters

Now that I am in my dotage I am often asked, by younger hill persons, if I have any nobbles, wrinkles or instant karma type wisdoms I can give them vis-à-vis the great outdoors. Here in no particular order are the rules of thumb that have kept me (relatively) out of mischief in the mountains.

* Wear two pairs of socks all the time. Even in bed. I don't know why, it just seems to make sense.

* Change your underwear every day. If you can't then beat it with a stick. (Remembering to take it off of course). This is an old trick I learned from Baden Powell's *Scouting For Boys*. (True).

* Keep your toenails cut short if you plan on using a Lilo.

* If you are trekking in a Muslim country never poke fun at a Djinn; there are lots of three inch tall trekkers in freak shows around the Middle East who should have known better. The same goes for Africa and witch doctors. In England however you can poke fun at ordinary doctors – but don't expect them to treat you when you go in with an ice axe in your head.

* Talking of which, never drink while in control of an ice axe; look what happened to Trotsky.

* Talking of which, if you do get the trots while in a foreign clime then run: it's faster than trotting and it helps to avoid embarrassing social moments.

* Remember that it is impossible to cough or sneeze while still retaining control of the anal sphincter: so if you do have the trots, pray to whatever God you believe in that you do not also get a cold. I know – I was that soldier: Kathmandu, October 1992.

* If you get the trots really bad then the only answer is three of sand and one of cement.

* If you get blisters shout at them. Let them know who's

boss. Shout things like, 'Call that a blister! I had one in the Adirondaks that was bigger than an ostrich egg.' If that doesn't work, sing to them. I usually find that a few verses of *The Ball of Kerrimuir* or the duet from *The Pearl Fishers* sorts the problem out. If all else fails there's not much really that you can do except cut your feet off. If you do this remember to have some stump oil handy – it will make the rest of your walking day so much more pleasant.

* Remember that what is acceptable in some cultures is not acceptable in others. E.g. consuming vast amounts of the Earth's resources while becoming fat, aggressive, ignorant and wearing Chav gear may be *de rigeur* in the West, but is actually thought to be pretty stupid in some parts of the Himalayas. The same goes for walking through tribal areas while wearing shorts that show your bum chins.

* Keep a journal. It may never get published but it will give the grandchildren something to laugh at in future years, particularly if you illustrate it with your own photographs.

Look at Granny in that Day-Glo spandex. She looks like a light bulb! Look there's the last picture of Grandad in Nepal hanging on the edge of that crevasse. There's Granny behind him with the insurance policy.

* Never trust any animal that can move faster than a rock, that has teeth, that has feet or paws bigger than a mouse, that stings, or that knows all the words to any national anthem.

* Never drink at altitude if there's a vowel in the month.

* If you're going to have sex in the mountains make sure that you are belayed to something, and not just to each other.

* Remember, it's a long road that has no turnips.

* If there's a bull or other nasty thing in a field, wear Marks and Spencer's clothing, and try and be bad at what you are doing. The last thing you want to be is outstanding in your field.

* Talking of bulls – here's an easy way to spot a dangerous bull from a non-dangerous bull. The non-dangerous bull is the one with the rubber horns.

* While trekking in the Himalayas – if you do find Shangri La remember that, if you come out later, not only will you have grown older, but your library book will be overdue and your council tax will stand at seventeen trillion pounds.

* If you get homesick while you are far away then sit down calmly and think about home. Remember the mortgage, the dripping tap, the wet bit under the bath where the boards are going, the gutter above the garage that needs mending, the pointing that needs doing where the gutter has been leaking, the ceiling in the dining room that needs re-plastering, the worn carpet on the stairs, the door that has fallen off the kitchen unit because the hinge has broken, the garage full of broken strimmers, punctured space hoppers and unused exercise bikes.

Then think of the kids: all the money they are costing you; the way they look at you and either roll their eyes at your stupidity or pull a face as though you are something they've just trod in. Then think how they will grow up into ungrateful selfish buggers that will put you in a home at the first sign of dribbling or puddles under the chair; (it wasn't me, it was the dog!) then will sell your house, and then never come and visit you. I guarantee that soon you will not feel homesick at all.

* And finally: if you go trekking in a developing country (what's developed about us I would like to know with our germ warfare, reality television and oven-ready meals?) don't give the children sweets, toys or empty plastic water bottles: give them a new school, a clean well, or a health centre.

May, 2005

Bilbo Baggins We Hates It, Cluck, Cluck

I only realised how dangerous our sport/ pastime/ distraction/ hobby/ whatever, is the other day when I read about a poor woman out walking who was knelt on by a cow and killed. It seems that she had a dog with her.

Now not too many people know this, but dogs and cows do not get on with each other. Cows naturally (and probably quite rightly) assume that all dogs are up to no good. As somebody who has been bitten by several dogs in the course of my lifetime, all of whose owners claimed, '*He's only playing,*' I too always assume the worst of any dog. Compared to cats, dogs are smelly, stupid and dangerous. Cats don't crap on the pavement, they go into somebody's garden and dig up their dahlias to make a nice latrine. You don't get cats guarding scrapyards then running amok in a playground full of children tearing them to pieces. And cats won't run for a stick if you throw it them; cats are far too intelligent for that. As far as they are concerned it's your stick, you threw it, you fetch it.

So, if you are going into a field full of cows with a dog then, unless the dog has a machine gun, an anti-tank grenade, or a small nuclear device in its back pocket, it should get out of that field ASAP. Should the cows decide to come and investigate, then let it off the lead and disown it. Point to the dog and say, 'It's not mine – it's been following me all day. I hate dogs.' If you're lucky and aren't a New Labour politician the cows might just believe you.

I have, on occasion, taken dogs walking with me. When I was more fixed of abode, and lived in one place for longer than three hours I had two dogs in succession. The first was really my daughter's dog called Sam (AKA Samantha) who I bought from a one-lunged, Geordie sound engineer who used his remaining lung to inhale copious amounts of Jamaican herbal tobacco which he took for premenstrual cramps. (Every word true.)

Sam was an Old English Sheepdog with incredibly bad eyesight and the firm, if unfounded belief, that people's crotches had something in them which, if only she could nuzzle it out, would contain the secrets of the universe, or at least God's mobile phone number. She was lovely to look at but not very bright, a sort of Sloan Ranger of the dog world. Her memory span was that of an educationally sub-normal goldfish, so that every walk was a totally new experience to her. This meant that stiles were a constant and difficult learning experience for her. She would just about get the hang of them by the end of one walk; then her memory chip would self erase, so that the next time you took her out she had no idea what stiles were, and had to be hauled over them like an old, gouty matron.

I took her on a hike over Ingleborough one hot summer's day. It was supposed to be a short walk but the cloud came down, I got us lost for a couple of hours and added several miles to the walk. When we finally made it down into Ingleton, hours later and both of us footsore and bushed, she hid under the settle of the pub and refused to come out until I promised her a car ride back home. After that she decided that mountains were not for her and took to hiding whenever I got a map out; from that day on, boots were to her what garlic is to Dracula.

When Sam went to that great lamp post field in the sky, Billy (my daughters named him Bilbo Baggins but I refused to call him that) arrived in the kitchen one night in the person of an almost-pedigree, Jack Russell terrier pup from the local dogs' home. Almost-pedigree? Whatever his mother had been crossed with must have been a combination of burglar, escapologist and comedian, because Billy was certainly a dog of rarity. He was actually quite well behaved, and would walk to heel most of the time. He never went near sheep, and would be across a field full of cows before they knew he'd been in it. But like all heroes he had paws of clay – his was chickens. Like the smell of a tap-room to a drunk on a hot summer's day, the scent and noise of chickens spelt out the letters, *P-A-R-A-D-I-S-E* to Billy.

On one walk with Billy, our route off the hill at the end of a long day took us through a farmyard. I was busy taking photographs when I heard the noise of affronted egg layers, and turned the corner to see Billy in amongst a lot of hens. The birds, terrified by this rampant ball of fur and teeth on legs were all trying to get into the hen-house at the same time, and were jammed in the little door in best Tom and Jerry cartoon tradition.

I managed to get him to heel just as the farmer's wife came running round the barn end in wellies and an apron.

'Has your dog been at my chickens?' she asked quite angry, and justifiably so.

'No, not him' I lied. 'He never chases chickens. He won't go near them. He's terrified of them.'

It was at this point that Bilbo Baggins coughed up two generous, handfuls of chicken feathers.

The woman looked at me.

'He must have swallowed a pillow,' I said weakly as Billy looked up at us grinning and wagging his tail like a dog with two tails.

October, 2003

Feminist Walks in Taliban Country

I was in Waterstone's on Deansgate, Manchester, the other day wandering round their excellent travel section looking at the climbing and walking books when, like Paul on the road to Damascus, I was hit by the Tripoli bus, figuratively speaking. First of all I was struck by the fact that the walking books seem to have been breeding and that, like planarian worms, it was difficult to tell them apart; then I was struck by the fact that most of them when not about dead people like Mallory and Shipton seemed to be about people who had nearly bought the farm, cows, mangle bodger and all.

There seem to be six new books a month written by people who have lost bits of their body to frost and ice while on the north west ridge of Kwangedunga or Chomolinctus or Sharmikebab or some such; and another half dozen every month by people who fell down things or off things, and had to crawl out again with no legs and arms using their eyelashes and tongues. It does make going anywhere other than down the local B and Q for a cordless drill seem an irrevocable sentence of death, or at the very least means that when you do get back from your expedition, you will have to go on your lecture tour with several attendant nurses, and give your lecture from the comfort of a large bucket. It seems to me that either things are becoming much more dangerous, or that people seem to feel that they have to burden us with their problems more. I'm not sure that I like this kind of confessional mountain writing.

Now when I was a lad, and did a lot more than I do now, you didn't talk about it; you got on with things. We wouldn't have got to where we are today if we had all been moaning minnies. If things fell off, you shoved them in your pocket, and just got on with it hoping that you'd find a quiet moment in camp, after the cocoa, when the embers had been kicked and the wood sparks were making swirling galaxies on the sky's bosom, to approach the Doc and quietly whisper in his ear, man to man, as you knocked your pipes out on a coolie's head.

'Don't want to trouble you Doc, but one of me old feet fell off on the march this morning and I was wondering if you had any of that medical type glue I could stick it back on with? Don't open a tube specially for me though, I can wait till you've a couple of things you need to stick back on.'

I remember reading once how Shipton and Tilman almost came to blows arguing about how many shirts you needed for an expedition of three months; whether it was two, or whether one would do. I also remember reading in *A Short Walk In The Hindu Kush* how Wilfred Thesiger watched Eric Newby and his companion blowing up their lilos in the Hindu Kush and snorted. 'Hmm – couple of poofdahs,' before lying down on the stony ground and rolling the hardest boulder he could find under his head to use as a pillow. Those were the days were they not, when aftershave was a handful of steaming yak dung, and you pulled your own teeth out with a pair of cobbler's pliers.

Another thing I don't like about the new mountain writing is the confessional psycho babble note that has crept in, due I suppose to those atrocious television programmes where couples go on in front of the camera, and the lorry driver husband with muscles in his spit tells the world, and his wife, how he likes to dress up in black suspenders and stockings, a leather thong, a Wonderbra and a Marks and Spencer's size eighteen cocktail dress and go sitting amongst the matrons at the local bingo hall. Then the wife's brother runs on and thumps him, because that's what he has always wanted to do.

What I suppose I am trying to say in a roundabout way is that people's peccadilloes seem to me to be like Widnes and Solihull: I know where they are but nothing in the wide world would ever make me want to go there.

I am not interested if tensions arose between an expedition

leader and some of the group who felt that he wasn't the right man for the job because he ate more than his fair share of the porridge on the walk in; I don't care if camp three aren't talking to camp four because they cheated at Scrabble, and I don't care if nobody is talking to the expedition cook because they found his glass eye and his jock strap in the soup.

It's more important that people pull together and follow the leader and do as they are told. And, if things go wrong and people die or otherwise get upset, then that's just the way things are, and it's no use being a load of moaning minnies like that little William Hague. You have to be strong like Mrs Adolph Thatcher or General Pinochet.

The other thing that struck me in the bookshop is how many different kinds of walks you can do. I mean apart from up a hill and down again, or away from your car in a circle round the hills and back again, you can do pub walks, walks up hills more than 3,000 feet high, walks with the family, walks along old railway tracks, walks with the family to pubs up mountains over 3,000 feet high along old railway tracks, walks along pilgrims' routes, smugglers' routes, double glazing salesmen's routes – quite amazing, the list is curtailed only by one's imagination.

As soon as I finish this article I am going to start on a series of books that will make me a fortune: *Pub Walks In Utah*; *Feminist Walks in Taliban Country*; *Walking the Norfolk Munros* – I feel that I am at the beginning of a new career. All I need now is a publisher daft enough.

December, 1999

I Wandered Lonely as a Cow

There is a bench by the roadside in Horton in Ribblesdale, just across from the Pen y Ghent café. It was put there a few years back by a group of hill walkers and cavers from the Burnley area in memory of one of their group who had loved the Three Peaks region, and who had died young. It has a simple inscription on the back rest, *I came to the Hills and they welcomed me.* Somewhere on a Lakeland mountain once I came upon a small aluminium cross with, these lines etched onto it,

Great things are done when Men and Mountains meet
They are not done by walking in the street.

Remembering these lines the other day got me to wondering about the poetry of the Great Outdoors. *Pastoral, mystic, green,* call it what you will, there is a whole Golden Treasury of verse out there inspired by the hills, the mountains and the wild places of the world, and if any publisher of poetry anthologies is reading this then please consider me for the job of editor of *The Faber Book of Wilderness Verse.*

We could begin with Anon, starting perhaps with that wonderful Anglo Saxon poem:

Whan sumer is y cumin in
Cuku lude sing.
Men taken oot theyre boots and soks
An gan a ramblouring.
With maidens to ye woods they goo
Eek finden mossy bonk,
And in the merry greenwoods they
Hey nonny nonny nonk.

After a few pages of Anglo Saxon anonymous poetry we would come to Chaucer and his *Canterbury Tales* with the wonderful Boy Scouties Tayle:

Wan Aprile with his shoores soothe
The very earth has drenched to the roote,
Then gan the scooties on their jambouree
With baggie shoorts and nabbly nabbly knee.
Whilom was one yclepped Jason,
With fayce eek like a pudden basen.
A trainee spotter's braine y had,
Theis warty, spottey, littil lad.
One nighte in ye quatermaster tent
O'er the suet Jason bent,
This yunge ladde to his greete sorrow
Eftstoons forgot the scooties motto,
And ye noughtie scoote maister took him unawares
Forre Jason didde forget to 'Be Prepared'

A short leap forward in time to the Metaphysicals brings us to John Donne and his wonderful *To A Midge* written while on a camping holiday in the West of Scotland, in which the poet uses the conceit of the rapacious midge to seduce his loved one.

Mark but this midge,
And mark in this,
How little that what thou denyst me is.
It first sucked me and now sucks thee
And in this midge our two bloods mingled be.
How can this be said
A shame or loss of maidenhead?
So get thy kit off while I have the notion,
To rub thee with some calamine lotion.

Milton, Shakespeare, Willie (Whacky Baccy) Wordsworth, all of them at some time have flung their three groats' worth of verse at the Great Outdoors, and who can forget *The Rhyme of the Ancient Rambler* by Samuel Taylor Coleridge?

It is an ancient Rambler
He stoppeth one of three,
'By thy long grey beard and glittering een
Now wherefore stoppest thou me?

On Kinder Scout when all about
Are mists and fog? By heck!
In this bog and moss an Albatross
Is hung about thy neck!

Thou art a louse! To shoot a grouse
Is bad but this is worse.
To shoot an Albatross will bring
Upon thy head a curse.'

'God wot I shot it not! I bought
It at Marks and Sparks you dunce
Tandoori Albatross with nan
Thou wazzock this is my lunch!

Coming to the poets of today, we could finish the book with Roger McGough's poem for kids, *Walker's Crisps:*

They sell Walker's Crisps at our corner shop
It's said they taste a treat,
But can you see it puzzles me
What do cyclists eat?

(Answer: Saddle of Lamb)

Enquiries from interested publishers particularly if accompanied by Martin Amis type advances will be very welcome.

Now, before I go, I'm going to tell you something that is absolutely true. If you think everything else I have ever written is rot, and believe nerry a word of it, then believe this.

Wordsworth, one of our first (though not, in my opinion, one of our best) mountain writers opened an early draft of the daffodil poem thus:

I wandered lonely as a cow
That roams about on dale and hill
And all at once I saw some flowers,
And do you know they were daffodils!

And thus it would have remained had not his sister, Dorothy, said, 'You can't write that you great wazzock! Change it to, cloud. And he did. And that is absolutely true.

August, 1999

Congestion Charges on Snowdon

I suppose it's of little interest, but I've had an eye operation recently; nothing serious, just a bit of digging and scraping and stuff. As a result of this op, my eyesight is now perfect in my right eye, but as bad as it ever was in my left eye. This has resulted in me walking round in circles, and offers of a part in the Hartlepool Panto, *Treasure Island,* as Long John Saliva, starring opposite Jordan as Robinson Crusoe. I don't fancy having my leg off, and am allergic to parrot crap, so I have decided to decline their kind offer.

The operation has meant that, for the first time in years, I have been able to walk in the hills without having to wear glasses; which means no steaming up on the inside, and no rain on the outside. I do have to pick my mountains carefully though, and have begun to favour very round mountains so I can end up back where I started from (and cries of Polyphemus do greet me wherever I go – which is disconcerting). In the New Year I will get the other one done and then I can walk in straight lines up mountains instead of having to go around them. Which brings me to the main point of this little bit of gibber.

I came off a round mountain the other evening, and made my way into the pub for a wet. As I was drinking my pint of Old Gunghapooch India Pale Ale, I heard a local landowner of some note (I think it was C Sharp) say that, because of the recent fall in farm incomes, it would be a good idea if they put turnstiles at the bottom of the hills and charged people to walk up them.

I am not a violent type and my eye was still hurting, so I said nothing, but this is what I thought to myself: *a man like that should have his brains confiscated and locked away in a dark cupboard until he is old enough to handle them, small as they may be.*

Some of you gentle readers will know that Harding's *History Of England* contains a whole chapter on how (in this country at least) the land we walk upon as outdoor types was snatched from the Common People and taken into the hands of the few in one of the biggest heists in history, so that what was once a country of little farmsteads and open country became a land of large estates girt round by iron laws. This went on for centuries until all most of us have is the land our house is built on and enough over for a swing and a paddling pool for the kids.

And now, the upshot of it all is that the people who ripped the land off us in the first place, are thinking seriously of charging us to walk on it. Of course it's no different from the Mad Grannie of Grantham who took the water boards created by the great city corporations (paid for by the ratepayers of those cities) and sold them off to her cronies – who then sold them off to Anglo-French Utilities Inc. who were then taken over by International Gromets and Gussets Plc. Haweswater and Thirlmere are now owned by Donald Rumsfeld's sister's hamster (I made that bit up, but it's probably not far from the truth).

Anyway, the logical conclusion – to which turnstiles on mountains leads me – is to toll pavements. Why should it just be the mountains? Why don't we have toll booths on the pavements so that we can charge people to walk on them? We could license the pavements to a new PFI to be created by the Blessed Blair to be called, FootTrack. Monitors would log every yard you walked and deduct it automatically from your earnings, after you've paid off your student loan, your private Foundation Hospital Medical Insurance and your Aircon charges. Aircon? Come on! It's only going to be a matter of time before they have a PFI to charge us for the air we breathe! Each of us, at birth, will be fitted with a flow meter and a transmitter so that every c.c. of air we breathe can be logged and charged to us. Any last breaths we take on our deathbeds will be charged to our dependents at 19% APR.

They've already privatised the earth and the water, why should the air be exempted? Fire would be a bit more tricky since that's a slippery sort of element, but I'm sure New New Labour will find a market-force, trickle-down way round it.

So, let us suppose they get away with it and put turnstiles at the foot of every hill and mountain, and toll booths on every road into our National Parks – don't laugh, they charge you to get into cathedrals now courtesy of Prayercon Inc – (Our Motto Penance Per Pound Paid) so the hills will be easy peasy.

Of course there will be the protesters like me who will leap the turnstiles, and chain ourselves to a bit of Crib Goch, or Coniston Old Man – but we'll be labelled Loony Lefties and Anti-Patriotic and Tree Hugging Saddam Lovers by the *Daily Mail* and the *Express*, while the *Times* letters page will be filled with letters questioning why the turnstiles have been made in Italy when there are perfectly good British turnstile makers. One letter will be from somebody saying they couldn't hear the first cuckoo this year because of squeaky foreign turnstiles.

I remember once somebody telling me that I shouldn't be so political in my writings and my stage and television comedy. It reminded me of all those priests who told me, when I was a child and still frightened of them, that God was in heaven and all was right with the world.

Well God may well be in Her Heaven, but she's obviously busy with the housework, because the chancers and crooks are getting away with it again, and until God finishes whatever it is that's keeping Her busy it's up to us to do something about it. For, trust me, as long as the Blessed Blair is there with his magic PFI wand, there's a good chance we will end up with turnstiles on the hills. As my old Gran used to say, *They'd steal your eye and come back for the socket.* Hmm, Eyes? Sockets? Now, considering my op that's more than a bit ironic, n'est ce pas?

February, 2004

A Rough Guide to Rumpety Pumpety Al Fresco

I was quaffing a pint of Old Miasma in my local alcohol outlet site, the Duck and Rupture Truss a few nights ago, when one of the assembled company, Arthur Parrot, hill walker and climber and one time Barnsley lighthouse keeper, remarked that the recent long, hot summer reminded him of the time he and their lass had been courting, and were madly in love with each other, and had made love in the heather and soft couch grass of several moorland hills. Since Arthur and his missus have long been at that stage where saying, *Good Morning* to each other sounds like a declaration of war, we each of us reached into the dark cupboards of our imaginations to think of a time when Arthur could see his feet without a mirror, and his missus didn't have a mouth like a hen's ovipositor.

'It were grand. Open air lust. Tha can't beat it,' he told the ensembled crowd. 'We used to go out into the hills with us butties and flask, and find somewhere nice and quiet to sit down in the sun. Then, after the beverage that cheers had been imbibed, and the last crumbs scattered into the heather, one thing would lead to the other, and before you know it we would be engaged in full congress.'

'Isn't that a political meeting or something?' asked Sid Margolis, barber and prize Marrowfat Pea grower of this parish.

'No, he's talking about Rumpety Pumpety,' explained Barney Sullivan, ex-priest and the intellectual in our midst.

Well one thing led to another and before too long we were in earnest discussion as to the relative merits of heather, springy grass and moss, vis-à-vis open air Rumpety Pumpety.

Now let me tell the gentleman from Northern Ireland who writes repeatedly to me complaining about the bad language I use, and my tendency to wander away from things mountaineering into side alleys and cul de sacs, that the rest of this column will be devoted to matters rumpety pumpety al fresco, and that he should get his BIC pen and his Basildon Bond pad out now and write yet another badly spelled letter in stick writing to my editor Macaroon Camiknickers asking for me to be sacked. However I digress.

There were no great conclusions reached that night, and, as we said good night under the sputtering gas lamp, we agreed to differ as to whether heather or hay, pine branches or meadow fescue were the best beds for Passion's play. But it left me thinking about things and, later that night, after I had wound the cat up and put the alarm clock out, I got to cogitating.

Call me a romantic old fool if you like but I think that there can be no experience more akin to bliss than making love on a mountain top in high summer under a sunny sky on a soft grassy bed. With larks singing up above, the sun beating down on your naked limbs, and the person of your dreams (or at least somebody you know quite well) in your arms you are surely approaching the gates of some kind of terrestrial paradise? I am of course assuming that there are no troops of Boy Scouts wandering towards your love nest singing 'Gin Gan Gooly Gooly Gooly Watcher Goolies' and no ramblers in grubby macintoshes lurking behind a nearby rowan. I am also assuming that due care and attentivity have been taken vis-à-vis cow pats, stinging nettles and hedgehogs.

Reaching back into the dim recesses of my brain I remember walking hand in hand through the Blue Remembered Hills above Hardcastle Crags with a young lady I had met at a Methodist youth club. I was not a Methodist, having enough trouble and angst being a lapsed, short-sighted Roman Catholic, but the rock and roll band I played in, *Rocky and the Teen Beats*, had recently played at the youth club for a dance, and our eyes had met across a crowded room full of boys with sideburns and acne, and girls with padded, circle-stitched bras and ponytails. I was all of seventeen years while the lady in question, a red head with a large chest was a few months younger. I will not go into any more detail since I am finding it hard enough to type this stuff as it is without all the blood in my body leaving my brain and fingers to go to the antipodean bits, but let me, in best *News of the World* prose, tell you that one thing led to another and, while larks were carolling above, and a soft warm breeze was gently stirring the heather, we followed Passion's Path.

But as ever the Great Cosmic Jester was steadfastly on watch and, just as things were reaching what Robbie Burns called, *twa gae ups for ane gae doon*, I made a sudden lunge, slipped and rolled all my ten stone of naked cherubic flesh into a large patch of stinging nettles. The dance I executed on that moorland top would have made a whirling dervish look like a moribund tortoise, and any thoughts of further dalliance went out of the window for, not only was I stung, smarting and swollen, but my red haired friend had laughed so much that she had given herself a nose bleed. However we did progress in the weeks of that long hot summer to discover that though heather gives more bounce to the ounce, the long soft stems of meadow fescue make a perfect couch for what Arthur Parrot termed *congress.*

This combination of hill walking with the carnal is one that I am sure will be familiar to more than a handful of fellow mountaineers (I know at least one fellow mountain journalist who has made love on top of Mullaghmor in the Burren of County Clare) and I often wonder whether there ought not to be a *Rough Guide To Rumpety Pumpety Al Fresco*, not that I am in the way of writing such a tome myself you understand, it's just that it would give another dimension to the walking world. Jake Thakeray once wrote a song about a girl who made love on national monuments, it would be quite nice if there was a league for people who had made love on every hill over two thousand feet. You could even have a medal struck showing a discarded brassiere and a pair of Y-fronts dangling from a trig point. One thing you would have to watch out for though is paragliders. Unlike Gin Gan Goolying Boy Sprouts, they are silent as the breeze, and you only know they are there when a cooling shadow falls across your naked botty, and you hear somebody calling down, 'Funny place to do press ups.'

October, 1997

Zeus Was Out – Part One

Beware of Greeks bearing mountains, my old gran used to say as she sat there in her rocking chair, sandpapering the budgie. Oh how I wish I had listened to her.

Readers of this mishmash of home truths, rant and surrealism will remember that a few chapters back I mentioned that I met Dimitri, a Mancunian-Welsh-Greek friend of mine who asked me to climb Mount Olympus with him. Those of you who were awake may also remember that I said yes. I should have been taken away there and then by the men in white coats to that nice hospital with the rubber rooms where everybody is gentle with you. Because here followeth a full and true account of what befelleth during those days even unto the third generation of lawyers, all of whom have had a good gander at the text in case of libel. The following is a true and honest transcript of my journal of those days spent climbing Greek's highest mountain and the abode of the gods – well a couple of them at least.

RETURN TO PARANOIA –
THE FIRST COMEDIC ASCENT OF METAXA –
SUMMIT OF MT. OLYMPUS 10,000FT AND COUNTING.

Day Minus One – Sleepless in Manchester

I arrive back in Manchester from Connemara at 4.30 pm and race to the YHA shop for a head torch and a Platypus water carrier, both of which I left in Connemara. No doubt the mice in the cottage will be having a high time playing with them now. I go to Waterstone's to hear Pete McCarthy reading from his book on Ireland, *McCarthy's Bar* which, like Pete, is very perceptive and very funny. After the reading we go for a pint and chat about

Ireland and the Irish. He's a nice bloke and we have a good old natter then, after a very abstemious two pints of Arthur Guinness's Best Black Mischief I go home to pack, leaving a pub before closing time for the first time since I was seventeen, and got dragged off by a loose woman from the sixth form of Notre Dame Catholic Girls School. I spend all night paying bills, sorting post out and packing, and finally crash at 1 am.

Day One – Take Me To Your Leda

I lie awake all night, my mind plagued with the thought that I have to be at the airport at 5.30 am. I try my hardest to sleep for the four hours until the taxi comes but can't. I am bedevilled with stupid fears: what if the alarm doesn't go off? What if the taxi doesn't come? What if they come knocking on the door for that library fine I never paid in 1958? What if I end up in the school playground wearing only a vest, and it doesn't cover my willy?

I doze off at 4.44. At 4.45 the alarm goes off. I shave my teeth and brush my face, dress erratically and adventurously in a Hawaiian shirt of the kind of pattern and hues that would induce an epileptic fit in a three toed sloth, drag on a pair of baggy walking pants, my boots and my Tilley hat and go downstairs to greet the dawn and the Pakistani taxi driver who asks me where I'm going. I assume that the controller has told him I'm going to the airport and think that he means where am I going ultimately.

'Mount Olympus,' I answer.

He looks for it in his A to Z of Manchester then asks if it's near the university. A few more misunderstandings later we head for the airport. I speak to him once or twice in the simple spirit of conservation, explaining that Olympus is where the Gods live but joke that they will probably be out.

'That Zeus is a real character. He's always getting dressed up as a swan and going off for a bit of rumpety pumpety with young Greek women.'

This I know as a fact from O-Level Eng. Lit. and Yeats' poem *Leda and the Swan.* I quote a bit at him.

A shudder in the loins engenders there
The broken wall, the burning roof and tower
And Agamemnon dead.

'That's the trouble with those Jerry builders innit?' he says. 'I saw a programme on them the other night yeah? They did this bloke's house up and the gable end fell down.'

'No this was a swan and because it had sex with this girl called Leda the Trojan wars started. And that's where I'm going: Mount Olympus via Terminal One.'

The taxi driver is now totally convinced that he is carrying a madman, and is really relieved when I load my trolley at the airport and vanish into a crowd of Northern Sun Seekers who are assembling for their annual two weeks of sun, sin, sand, sex and salmonella.

5.45 am Dimitri and Danny arrive. Dimitri is my friend the Greek taverna owner; Danny is his son, a tall, witty, twenty year old Jewish lad (his mum is Jewish and that makes Danny Jewish) who has the manners and mien of a gentle, young rabbi. So there we are, three men heading for a mountain; a Greek, a Jew and a lapsed Catholic Zen Buddhist Atheist with a serious Guinness habit.

I have a row with the check in girl who tells me our hand baggage will have to be weighed. She then tells us it is too heavy. It isn't what she says but the way she says it, as though we are all three of us puppies that have just crapped in her best hat. She is very pretty, but comes from one of the former Eastern Block states and has the manners of somebody who has been drummed out of the KGB for cruelty. I point out that two thousand pounds worth of cameras and lenses will not like travelling in the hold. She tells Dimitri I am shouting at her. I shout at Dimitri that I am not shouting at her, she is shouting at me.

I go off to cool down, and she shouts at Dimitri who has even more of a problem than me because his hand luggage contains a digital camera, a laptop computer, cables, chargers, batteries, etc. and a mobile camera to transmit pictures of us on the top of Mount

Olympus to the waiting world (actually the *Barnsley Bugle* and the *Manchester Echo*, a couple of free sheets where Dimitri advertises his Dolmades, Taramasalata and Bazouki Evenings). Dimitri puts most of his stuff through as hold baggage. I take my cameras out of my hand luggage, and put them round my neck. She weighs the lenses and they are ok. We get our boarding cards. I put my cameras back in the hand luggage and watch as our fellow passengers run for the duty free like passengers on the *Titanic* legging it for the lifeboats, as though they have heard that there will be no more booze and fags ever again, ever. Later they will stagger up the plane steps with several kilos of goodies each and try and cram this stuff into every available space: in lockers, under seats, between knees, up jumpers, in cheek pouches. What is it about duty free booze and fags? This stuff kills you – only cheaper. I suppose that must be the attraction.

After my row with Miss Bratislava 1999 we go for a coffee at one of the food places on the concourse. The coffee tastes of nothing – not bad, nothing. It is a vacuum, an absence of, a negation of taste. Dimitri gets mad about the coffee, and has a row with the café bar manager just to keep his hand in with the row business. So far Danny has had a row with nobody, and we tell him he'll have to buck his ideas up soon.

September, 2000

Zeus Was Out - Part Two

We land at Thessalonika where we are met by Tassos who is the brother of Nikos who works for Dimitri in the Manchester Taverna. Nikos has the mien of a young Greek monk, and the young Greek monk wants it back.

He introduces us to his wife and daughter then takes us to a seafood café in an old flour mill down by the docks and treats us to a wonderful meal which includes something called eggplant shoes. How do they get the shoes off the eggplants I wonder? Do the eggplants put up a struggle? Dimitri is driving so doesn't drink. Danny and I have a couple of circumspect glasses of excellent wine, and feel the glow of the holiday suffuse us already. The mists of Manchester are forgotten and we bask in the Greek sunshine, even though we are down the docks under an old grain silo. Tassos and his wife and little daughter wave us off, and we leave on our journey into the unknown full to the gills with eggplant shoes and other excellent Bubble nosh (Bubble is Manchester rhyming slang – Bubble and Squeak – Greek). The Greeks are amazingly hospitable people – like the Irish only with garlic.

We wobble off to our hire car, and set off for Litohoro our base for Olympus arriving as the afternoon sun strikes the mountains, and from the plain we see our goal the summit of Olympus, Mitikas – which I have re-christened Metaxa in honour of the very fine Greek brandy of that name, and also because I have trouble remembering names. (Shakespeare might have had a vocabulary of 400,000 words but what good did it do him? Where is he now I ask? Dead is the answer.) The summit of Metaxa is 10,000 feet above sea level, which is where we are now, and we aim to get to it in three days. From where we stand on the plain we can see quite clearly the fragmented summit with its great serried fangs. The temperature here on the plain is 34 degrees centigrade. It's going to be hot in that gorge: approaching forty.

We plan to walk the gorge to Prinoia where the road that runs above the gorge ends and then push on to the main refuge on the mountain the first day; spend a rest day on the hill, then go for the summit on the third day returning that same day to Prinoia where we can hitch a lift from the road head back to Litohoro. Sea level to summit and back in three days – easy peasy.

We check into the hotel have a quick souvlaki then go to sit in the town square with a beer to watch the world go by. I notice a raddled looking, non-Bubble type staggering round the square and go over to talk to him. It turns out that he's an American just back from Olympus. Strangely for an American he has bad teeth. In that land of the orthodontist and the whitewashed gnashers a man with teeth like a mouthful of dimps is as rare as an Eskimo with sunstroke. I ask him how long it took.

'We were kind of loose man. Took a lot of wine and a lot of grass with us. We kinda got lost for a while. Took us twelve hours to Paranoia (I decide that this is a much better name than Prinoia – and as it turns out much more fitting) and there was no way up or down so we slept out in the open. Like it was miserable, man. Then, man, we kinda walked to the refuge and stayed there two days, we were like so out of it. They were so sorry for us they gave us a map for free. Then like we went to the summit.'

I had heard various stories about the extent of exposure on the last pitch to the summit and ask him how it was.

'Man I held on with everything I had and three, four times I just froze on and prayed. No way am I ever going to take my ass back up there.' And he wanders off across the square. I saw him later on the balcony of his hotel with a couple of other Americans smoking what looked like rolls of wallpaper, and drinking bottles of retsina.

I go back to Dimitri and Dan, and take out the guide book. It's written by Tim Salmon, one of the excellent series of guides published by Cicerone. The last pitch is described as a *moderate scramble.* I say nothing to the others. We buy fruit, nuts and bottles of water from a late night store and go to our rooms to pack and make ready for the morning and our assault on the Mountain Of The Gods.

Day 2 Egg Lollies

The man in the next bedroom has been up all night taking showers and turning the television on and off in his unofficial capacity as facilities tester for room eleven. I emerge red eyed and trembling from my pit at 7 a.m. after a second sleepless night.

The landlady brings breakfast which is some bread and honey, a couple of hard boiled eggs that have been kept in the freezer so that they are now egg lollies, and a glass of reconstituted orange juice. (This in a country that is sinking under the weight of its fresh oranges.) I bang on the door of Danny and Dimitri's room to hear answering grunts. Either they have been eaten by bears or they are not happy campers first thing in the morning.

By 8 a.m. they have eaten their egg lollies, we have paid the landlady, left some kit in storage under her stairs, and set off walking out of Litohoro. We follow the high street out of the village passing the town cemetery where an old lady pulls on a bell rope tolling a dirge as we walk past. I see this as an omen. I am later proved right.

We follow an aqueduct for a while then meet two men on a bridge who point out a shepherd's trail into the forest. The sun is hammering down, the temperature already in the mid thirties. We look back at Litohoro and, further off, the wine dark sea of Homer far behind us. Still no sign of any big swans. Before us lies the gorge and at its head the fangs of Metaxa, as we enter the gorge, like Ariadne on the brink of love, we hear the bells of the cemetery still tolling

October, 2000

Zeus Was Out – Part Three

With the bells of the town graveyard still ringing behind us we drop down into the Litohoro gorge. The early morning sun is already hot enough to fry eggs on the pavement, but having brought neither eggs nor pavement we carry on walking and sweating. The heat in the gorge thickens as we climb steadily in its narrow confines going from close to sea level to where the old shepherd's track we are on enters a narrow stone gate on the cliff face. From here there are great views of the gorge ahead and the coast and town behind us. Having gained this height we lose a good lump of it again dropping back to river level. The temperature now must be close to forty with not a breath of breeze, and for hours we follow a switchback path along the river's bank. I am lathered in sweat, and though I'm drinking a lot of water it doesn't seem to be enough, and I can feel the beginnings of cramp in my calf muscles.

In two places the path leads out across the cliff face high above the river. Over the winter the path has fallen away, and twice we have to shuffle along twelve inches of crumbling dust with a lot of nothing underneath us. Dimitri is very quiet at both these points while Dan mutters phrases in Yiddish that have words in them like, *shnorrer, shlemiel* and *meshuganah.*

After three hours we stop for a food and water break at a side valley where a winter avalanche has carved a new gully into the gorge. There is a stream and a waterfall with tufa formations on the rock similar to those in Gordale Scar in the Dales and we sit for an hour rehydrating and eating our nuts and fruit. Once he's full of fruit and nuts, Dan decides that being the first junior rabbi on Mount Olympus isn't such a bad idea. Dimitri has a quick snooze, and I eat a bag of dried apricots, remembering too late that it was eating a bag of dried apricots in the Pakistan Himalayas that earned me the title amongst the Balti porters of 'the sahib with the exploding trousers.'

After the gully the path is more difficult, with boulders and fallen trees blocking our way forward. Most people climbing Olympus ignore the Litohoro Gorge, and go straight to the road head at Paranoia. Spending the day in an airless gorge scrambling over landslides in a temperature of forty degrees centigrade was my idea, which is why I am a *meshuganah shnorrer.*

Danny is going strong now over the difficult terrain. I'm much slower, and Dimitri is finding the going a lot harder. He's climbed Snowdon and Kinder recently but his only other climbing has been up and down the stairs in his Manchester taverna, and this is the first time he's carried a heavy pack. I've had some kind of a virus infection just prior to leaving for Greece which I've managed to defeat with echinacea tincture but I'm not on best form, so I too am finding it hard going. I've drunk a lot of water but have lost more through sweating in the unforgiving heat and, about an hour beyond the gully, I cramp up badly. At one point I have to lie flat out on a large boulder, both calf muscles locked solid, the pain so bad I describe it in my journal as, *like giving birth with your legs.* After bearing down and doing my breathing exercises I manage to carry on. For the next two hours I hobble on slowing everybody up.

We have not seen a soul all day, then suddenly twelve German walkers appear upstream, powering down towards us, their trekking poles flashing in the sun, all but two of them are women, mahogany brown and fit as butchers' dogs. The two men trail behind them. I ask them how far it is to Paranoia. They are not in the mood for talking but hurry on down shouting back over their shoulders, 'Not far – maybe one hour.' The guide book reckons the gorge should only take four and a half hours. It's three o'clock now which means we three *shlemiels* have been *shlepping* for seven hours, (six if you deduct the water stop) and are still an hour off Paranoia.

We plod on up the gorge. Dan mutters something about Moses

and forty years in the wilderness. Dimitri is too knackered to mutter. I mutter anyway just to keep Dan company.

A little way on we come to a chapel built into an overhang under the cliff where a stream springs from the rock wall, flowing through the chapel before falling down to the river. Inside the chapel an oil lamp burns before a handful of icons of Jesus and the Virgin Mary. One of the icons shows a nativity scene. Danny asks what it is. I tell him it's the first Christians' Holy Family and they are in a stable.

'Typical gentiles,' he says. 'They're living in a stable, but they spend a lot of gelt having their picture painted.'

I know this is an old joke but I still laugh.

We climb on up the gorge and a kilometre beyond the chapel we see a ruined monastery amongst the fir trees on the opposite side of the gorge. Dimitri looks in the guide book.

'The German's destroyed it because the Greek partisans were using it as a base.'

'No wonder they were in a hurry to get down,' Dan says, referring to the trekkers who had just gone down the trail.

'It was nearly sixty years ago,' Dimitri tells him.

'They didn't look that old,' Dan replies, innocently.

Dimitri and I look at each other, and wonder whether he's just pretending to be daft. We decide to leave it. The path is much easier now, and a slow and steady pace brings us to the little taverna at the road head at Paranoia exactly eight and a half hours after setting off. We are all completely trashed so any thought of going on the extra two and a half hours to the refuge on the mountain goes out of the window.

We sit and drink, rehydrating in the shade, and Dimitri manages to cadge us a lift back to Litohoro with a swarthy brigand-like character who drives a small truck up here every day bringing supplies for the mountain huts. Beyond Paranoia everything goes on mules.

I watch our driver-to-be throwing ouzo and beer down his throat as though he has heard a rumour that there is soon to be a world shortage of both commodities, and I wonder whether we shouldn't walk back. Greek mountain roads are bad enough with a sober driver – this guy is completely blootered, out of his tree, a danger to shipping and low-flying aircraft.

I silently curse the pope for demoting St Christopher from saint to ordinary mister, and watch in silent terror as our driver-to-be throws another glass of ouzo and another pint of beer down his gullet. He wipes his mouth, belches so loud that a donkey across the gorge mistakes it for a mating call and spends the next half hour answering back. Then our driver-to-be burps once more and falls off the bench onto the dusty floor spark out. We look at each other glumly. Here we are in Paranoia in a beer hut; no beds, a drunk driver, and a long, long journey back down the mountain to start all over again tomorrow.

'Oi gevalt,' Dan says which I think is Yiddish for something very bad.

November, 2000

Zeus Was Out – Part Four

They pick our driver up of the floor, dust him down and give him another ouzo and bottle of beer in case he has a sudden attack of sobriety. I ask Dimitri what the Greek is for, *We have changed our minds. We will sleep on the pile of mule crap outside. Please do not trouble the lorry driver any more.* But at that moment two and a quarter Germans arrive in the hut. The two are man and wife, the quarter is their four year old son, and they have just returned from climbing most of the way up Olympus. The last stretch was too dangerous for the child so they have turned back and are on their way down. Their car is parked here at the road head, they offer us a lift back down the mountain road and, after a nanosecond's hesitation, we accept. With profuse apologies to our Greek driver who is on the floor again, we pile in the back of the German's camper-van, and in an hour we are back at the little hotel we left this morning. I decide that Einstein must have worked out his Theory of Relativity while climbing a Greek mountain. How can it take less than an hour coming down and all day going up?

The landlady laughs like a drain, and gives us our rooms back. She knew we weren't going to make it. So why didn't she tell us, and save us all that trouble? I notice that she is wearing stockings held up just under the knee by rubber bands, and I also notice that she has a hairy mole on her chin. *Ha,* I think, *I might not be able to climb mountains, but at least I don't have a hairy mole on my chin or wear stockings held up by rubber bands.*

We have some food and go to bed glum as three buckets, deciding that tomorrow we will be real mountaineers and not shnorrer nebbishes who take all day to do the Litahoro Gorge. In the room above mine the Americans who stumbled up the mountain a few days ago on a diet of red wine and marijuana are smoking more dope, and drinking more red wine, and arguing about which country they are in. They finally decide that they are in Finland. I shout at them to shut up in German, then French, then Irish, and the debate starts all over again.

Day 3 Barking Teutonic Sphincters

In the morning the landlady gives us some more ersatz orange juice and egg lollies, and we set off again for the mountain. This time we drive to the hut at Paranoia following the hairy road above the gorge, avoiding the mountains of mule crap that are not marked on the map. We park beside the hut and gird our loins, all three of us in good heart. It is 8.30 and cool, the sun just edging over the rim of the gorge. The drunken driver-to-be is no longer on the floor of the shack so he's either in bed at home sleeping it off or at the bottom of the gorge, sleeping it off for a lot longer. We fill our water bottles and with a cheery disposition we enter the forest. Four hours and three thousand feet of walking later we arrive at the refuge, and are sitting in the sun on the benches outside the bunk house. Easy peasy this mountain climbing, we decide, just another three thousand feet-and-a-bit more, and we'll be on the top of Metaxa, the main summit peak of Mt. Olympus eating Ambrosia and talking to Zeus and Mrs. Zeus and all the other Greek gods and godettes.

Danny and Dimitri go for a lie down on their bunks while I sit in the sun watching climbers come and go. From the mountain refuge you can see all the way back to Litahoro and the coast, and all the way up to the serrated ridge of Metaxa which looks, from here, like the fingers of a gigantic splayed hand. A group of German blokes arrive heading upwards, very noisy and covered in dust and sweat. I hope they aren't billeted in our bunk room, then find out that they are.

Dinner is good and is cooked on wood fires fuelled by the windfall in the forests. After dinner we crash early ready for a dawn start and the climb ahead. As Danny and I lie on our bunks Dimitri starts to organise his pack taking (and this is no lie since I timed him) forty five minutes, during which, like some demented bag person, he shoves stuff in and out of plastic carrier bags. The bunk house is filled with the noises of somebody trying to be quiet and failing miserably. Plastic bags rustle no matter what you do, and after forty five minutes of Dimitri and the plastic bags, Danny shouts at him in Yiddish, and Dimitri gets back into his pit and all is quiet for three minutes.

Then the Germans come to bed. All night the Germans fart and whisper. The whispering is bearable but the farting is quite unbelievable: loud and long, unencumbered and widespread. For hours eight Teutonic sphincters bark and rasp in uncoordinated cacophony, and when one of them gets up to go to the toilet, lighting his way through the pitch-dark bunk house with a cigarette lighter, I half expect the refuge to be blown off the face of the mountain. I hate bunk houses and lie there sleepless and cursing, wondering what the hell I am doing climbing a mountain with a junior rabbi and a Manchester Greek taverna owner. Instead of counting sheep I secretly machine gun the trouser coughers in my imagination and soon the room is littered with the bodies of farting Germans.

Day 4 Up the Poo Staircase

The next day's journal begins:

Mein gott in himmel! Vas ein tag! Up at 5.30 to photograph the sunrise which is quite boring – without cloud the sun has nothing to play on and rises like an unpoetic orange balloon. The farting Germans come out too late, and just to get my own back I tell them that it was the best sunrise I have ever seen. They scratch themselves, fart some more and go back in to breakfast.

We pack and are off by 7 am. At first our way leads through forest and is a cool dander, then the forest thins out and gives way to rougher stony ground. Ahead of us Olympus beckons. Behind us we can see the Germans, a cluster of tiny farting dots following us up the mountain.

December, 2000

Zeus Was Out – Part Five

Once beyond the last straggling stands of the forest, we are in arid semi-desert conditions with the fanged peaks of Metaxa ahead of us, and the broad sweep of Kastro, another of the peaks of the Olympus range to our left. There are deep swathes of snow still lying in the gullies of Kastro; not many but enough to show how difficult these mountains can be earlier in the year. You have to wait until June or after for the snows to have cleared enough to make the mountains safe for ordinary hill walking. The farting Germans are gaining ground as Dan and I wait for Dimitri who is having difficulty with the temperature and the altitude. We're now approaching 9,000 feet. The altitude doesn't bother me because I'm not as tall as Dimitri.

The flies which are so much part of life in the forest, attracted there by the mountains of mule dung left behind by the pack trains, accompany us on our upward journey, climbing up our noses, clotting around our eyes, and generally making life miserable. We are above the tree line, not yet at the snowline, but obviously still well below the bluebottle line. The temperature is already in the top thirties and rising. Dimitri is not in his thirties and isn't rising; well he is rising, but gradually like soda bread. Dan as befits a young chap full of testosterone, lox and bagels is set fair to run to the top. I plod along at my usual pace, dripping with sweat and wild of hair, cursing the fact that I didn't have time to get my hair cut before I left, and realising that I now look like Ben Gunn on Treasure Island, the madman who spends his life looking for a bit of, *Christian bread and cheese* (what, I wonder, does Pagan bread and cheese – or Buddhist bread and cheese, taste like?)

The farting Germans who turned our night in the mountain hut into an unwanted but spectacular son et lumiere are now upon us.

Dan and I wait for Dimitri to catch up, and the Fahrtenwaffe zoom ahead of us towards the Cauldron and Kaki Skala. I had hoped the flies would follow them but they don't, they prefer us sweating English types.

I should explain here that Mount Olympus is really a massif of several interesting peaks, that look down into something called the Cauldron. The Cauldron is a huge corrie fifteen hundred foot deep and fringed at its western rim by the fangs of Mitikas, the main peak of the massif, some ten thousand feet above sea level. The ascent of Mitikas – or Metaxa as I re-named it – is described as a *moderate scramble* in our guide. A moderate scramble would, to me, describe something of reasonable difficulty, with three points of contact with the rock at all times and minimum exposure. It would also imply that the rock was stable. Hmm. Moderate scramble? I bite my thumb at you!

Anybody following the route that Dan and I took to the summit will see from the teeth marks on the rock that our interpretation of *moderate scramble* is different from the guidebook's.

When we get to the rim of the cauldron Dimitri lies on his belly, peers over the edge and looks at the way we have to go to make the summit, and says 'No'. This I decide is a pretty brave thing to do because any fool could say 'Yes', and then go on to climb beyond their ability. Which is what I do, because the next couple of hundred feet are pretty hairy, and consist mostly of me holding on to things while pretending to be brave. The route is named in the guides as the *Kaki Skala*. This is translated in some books as *Poor Staircase*. The true translation is *Shitty Staircase,* (check the dictionary) and in case you think I am making this up, it's there in black and white on the maps.

To get to the Kaki Skala we drop down off the Cauldron rim onto a crumbly arête that brings us to a traverse of several hundred metres of bad rock with a five hundred feet drop beneath us. When we get to the fangs of Metaxa there are two bad steps where we have to inch our way round spires of stone with a drop of five hundred feet on one side and fifteen hundred on the other. On the first of these Dan freezes on the rock, and I have no alternative but to climb round him and take the lead. After the second bad step we are in a broad gully with great slabs of rock and, every so often a clump of bright green grass.

Our tortuous way up this *moderate scramble* is marked with splashes of red paint put there by the Greek Mountaineering Club. They look too much like splashes of red blood for my liking. I send Dan ahead so that I can keep an eye on him, telling him to follow the red paint marks. Then I notice that he is going all over the place, scrambling erratically, climbing into impossible situations. I tell him to stop where he is and I take over the lead. I ask him what the hell he is doing not following the red paint marks: and it is at that moment just under the summit of Mt. Olympus that he tells me he is red green colour blind. He has been following the tufts of grass. What am I doing climbing Mount Olympus with a red-green, colour-blind junior rabbi? I ask myself. Luckily I don't answer.

I lead up some smooth slabs with poor holds that look as though they will be more of a problem on the way down, and by now I can see the Greek flag on the summit, and realise that we are going to make it – the first Joint/ Jewish/ Lapsed Catholic/ Buddhist/ Agnostic/ Manchester Olympus Expedition scrambles out of the gully and hugs each other. Then we drink some water, eat some chocolate, look at all the very deep holes around us and decide that it is no wonder the gods decided to live here.

There is no sign of Zeus. We ask one of the other gods, and he says that Zeus has probably gone off in his swan costume to give Leda another seeing to. We buckle our belts, stiffen our upper lips and set off down the mountain.

January, 2001

Zeus Was Out – Part Six – The Final Gasp

There is an old Yiddish proverb, *Gatkis shmekkle, reem, kaif chavver* which translates as 'What goes up must come down.' Danny and I had this very much in our minds as we said goodbye to the Greek Gods and crawled off the fragmented summit of Olympus. Since most deaths occur on descent; since only the previous week a Polish climber had gone to meet his maker down the Kaki Skala while descending from Olympus; and since Danny had a library book that he wanted to take back and didn't want the fines to accumulate as he lay in a Greek hospital bed with tubes sticking in him, we took extra special care on our way down.

Dropping down the gully, we descended a few hundred feet to the traverse, then singing songs to ward away the demons we girded our loins, didn't look down and scrambled back to the lip of the cauldron where Dimitri was waiting for us. By his side were four strangers, two couples in their twenties who had, like Dimitri, decided the summit ridge was too much for them. They applauded Danny and myself as we pulled up onto level ground.

'Do you speak any English?' I asked the strangers.

They shook their heads.

'They're Belgian,' Dimitri explained.

'Very nice chocolate, Tin Tin and Jacques Brel,' I said, smiling at the Belgians. They smiled back. Then I turned to Dimitri and gave him several minutes of very good Manchester cursing which included references to the fact that not only had he organised this trip, and left the fruit of his loins and myself to do the last nasty bit while he lay snoring in the sun, but that also he was a page boy at his parent's wedding, and not a member of Mensa; furthermore if he ever asked me to climb a mountain again two words not unconnected with sex and travel would spring to mind.

The Belgians laughed. They did not understand the words, but somehow the sentiment had communicated itself to them. Having got this off my chest we began the long descent. We had just climbed 3,000 feet, the last five hundred a severe scramble, and now had 6,000 feet of descent to make, most of it through piles of mule crap. I won't tire you with a blow by blow account of the heat, the dust, the flies that followed me down the mountain in clouds, licking the salt sweat off my skin, only leaving me when I came to a particularly fine pile of mule crap (so they preferred mule crap to me).

On we trudged, muttering and groaning in the heat; in the words of Captain Bloodnok, *It was Hell I tell you – no more curried eggs for me!* By the time we got to the road head we were hobbling like spavined frogs. (I don't know what a spavined frog hobbles like but it's a fair guess it looked like us.) Anyway oy gevalt! Enough already! We made it to the car with kneecaps exploding and boots on fire and drove immediately down the treacherous mountain track to Litohoro, where we staggered into the nearest Taverna after I had instructed Dimitri not to pass Go and not to collect two hundred pounds.

The first pint didn't touch the sides but fizzled and hissed when it reached the dry sandy bottom of my belly. The tavernist, or whatever it is you call a man who drives a tavern, didn't even ask us if we wanted any more, but brought three more tankards of chilled nectar toute suite.

'We Mount Olympus have just climbed,' I declared in fractured English.

'My twelve year old daughter did it on Sunday with her school,' he said in perfect English, smiling.

'He's lying,' I said to Dimitri as we got in the car to continue our pilgrimage. 'He has to be lying; either that or there's another smaller Olympus with steps up it.'

And so we bade farewell and aloah to the abode of the gods, and drove into the sunset heading for Meteora, our final destination, where we were to spend a few days of rest and recuperation looking at some monasteries that were built centuries ago on completely inaccessible rock pinnacles. Everything, including the monks had to be hauled up in baskets, and this isolation according to Danny, who is a student, served two purposes: being several hundred feet higher on a rock column sticking up off the plain brought you just that bit nearer to God so that you could meditate and pray in peace and silence; and it also meant that worldly distractions such as red-haired ladies with big bosoms, and Turkish marauders who wanted to chop your heads off, couldn't get near you. I suggest to Danny that they could have just hauled up the red-haired ladies with big bosoms and left the decapitating Turks far below. He thinks about it for a moment then says, 'In A.D. 786 Musselman the Devious Transvestite made his entire army of thirty thousand murderous muluks don red wigs and dress up in sheath dresses and fish net tights. Thus accoutred they got themselves hauled in baskets up all the rock column monasteries of Meteora, and decapitated all the monks. That's why even to this day there is a Greek proverb, *Beware red headed women with big bosoms bearing scimitars.*'

I tell him that not only do I not believe him, but that when we get to the Taverna we are staying at it as it's his round.

We drive through the soft evening light of Thessalonika dropping down to the plain of Meteora as night falls. After driving up a lot of dirt tracks where there is nothing but donkeys and prickly pears we arrive at the Koka Roka, our hostel for the night. It is built into the base of a massive rock with a monastery on the top. The landlady's son has spent thirteen years in Australia. He sounds like a cross between Harry Enfield's Stavros and Edna Everage. While he brings us beer his mum cooks chunks of lamb over an open fire, and, as the aroma of roast lamb and rosemary mingles with the scent of dust and lemon trees, the moon rises over the monasteries of Meteora, and our little Greek Oddity draws to a happy, if blistered, close.

February, 2001

Hang the Apple Macintosh!

When Mole in *The Wind in the Willows* decides that he has had enough, and he can't take any more, he throws down the whitewash brush, shouts, 'Hang spring cleaning!' and then goes off to have adventures with a rodent all-round good egg, and a spoilt aristocratic frog with a yen for fast cars and dressing up in washer-women's clothing. It's a little different when you spend all day working at a computer. After living much of the last six months writing a novel, chained to a typewriter like one of those proverbial monkeys who are supposed to be writing the works of Shakespeare, I can't exactly throw the Apple Macintosh through the window shouting, 'Stuff work! Bugger the novel!'

Apart from the fact that the falling Apple may well brain one of the cats, (neither of whom is called Newton) I'll still need the damn thing to do all the other things that living in End of Millenniaville entails: tax stuff, VAT returns, writing letters to the National Parks complaining about off-roaders and motorbike riders on bridleways, writing fan mail to La La in Tellytubbies – all the usual stuff. So the other day, on a late day in autumn that dawned with a low mist in the dale below me, covering the valley bottom like a lagoon of milk, odd islands of trees standing clear of the mist, and the first lick of sun clearing the fell's edge, turning the mist a pale gold, I metaphorically flung down the whitewash brush, switched off the computer I had been working at since six am., threw a bottle of water and some snap into my rucksack and, without a backward look at the VAT Cave, set off up the back lane towards the crag uttering purple prose like Wordsworth and De Quincey after a scrambled eggs and opium breakfast.

The lane to the crag is rough and stony, and my breath steamed in the cool air as I made my way past the deserted ruins of the last farm to be worked below the fell. Butterwort and lousewort spattered the bogland that lies in the hollow of the coomb, and sundew, its minute fronds beaded with dew was still there in small ruddy-green patches on the edge of the wettest bogs. Silurian stone stands in broken chunks and tumbled acres above the hollow, and I scrambled my way up through broken ground to the drystone wall that runs below the crag. The remains of an old stile still stand in the wall, just enough to get you over, so I crossed the boundary into open country and worked my way across the rake on the face of the scar.

I first saw this rake years ago when I came to live here and assumed that it was a footpath. It isn't. It is all that is left of an old pack horse way that leads over the fell northwards to Kendal and beyond. Looked at now it seems a strange way to go, travelling northwards when the most direct way is north west. But the jaggers way that the pack ponies took follows an older route first laid down when the valley bottoms were swamps, and the Romans weren't even a whisper on the wind. The Romans, when they came, used it as a quick way on to the fell, just as I was doing now, and once on the fell, followed an older, wider road across miles of open country to meet their marching road. That road is metalled now, but it still leads from the mouth of the Lune across leagues of hill country to Stainmore where men killed Eric Bloodaxe, King Of Orkney, King Of Dublin... but that's another story entirely.

From medieval days the rake was used to carry baskets of soft brown coal from the pits on the dales' flanks, across the fells to Kendal, where its high tar content and low burning temperature meant that it was prized by the tin smiths there because it worked the solder and the tin better than either black coal or charcoal.

I followed the way of the Romans and the soft brown coal up onto the head of the coomb, and stopped for a while to put a stone on a small cairn I have been building on the coomb's edge ever since I first came here. Cairn haters can take up their pens and howl, but men and women have been building cairns since the very beginning, and my small cairn just tells me the times I have been here, and marks the spot where I stand on the high point of the fell's shoulder each time, to look along the dale to its head and down the dale to its meeting with the Howgills, that great range of hills that rolls northwards to the lakes. From the cairn I followed a small stream over heather and gritstone outcrops to the bridleway. Before me – mile on mile of open fell cut by broad ghylls that lead northwards to the softer lands, flat green pasture lands rolling westwards to Lancaster, Morecambe and the sea. Close by the track to Lunesdale is a shepherd's shelter made of piled stones and roofed with slabs of the same material. The shepherds would come up here in the summer, living out with the flocks, driving them down to the valley for dipping, clipping and sheep sales.

I remembered the story of one old shepherd who looked after flocks on Blea Moor and Whernside in the Ribblesdale area. When he brought the flocks down from the hills to the farmers he worked for, he would collect his wages and then spend every penny in the Station Inn at Ribblehead, sleeping on the settle by the fire, drinking bitter beer and eating nothing but kippers which he bought by the box from a lorry driver who stopped at the pub on his way over to the eastern dales from the Isle of Man ferry at Heysham. Once the money was all gone he would gather up the flocks and drive them back up onto the fell for another few months. Victorian days? No – there are people alive who still remember him.

I left the shelter and re-traced my steps, heading for the higher ground above Barbondale. The stone walls that run from the valley bottom up seemingly impossible slopes to the fell summit were built in the late eighteen hundreds by men who slept out rough on the fell all week, gathering stones and fleshing out the walls with footings, throughs and top stones, working ten hour days, only going home at weekends. My friend's grandfather did it as a young man, for half a crown a week.

I had been away from home for an hour, walking, rambling, standing, looking. I sat in a sun trap where the last of the rowan berries burned in the sun, and had my snap. For the rest of that day

I rambled and mooched around, the only human being on the face of that fell noticing, for the first time a massive cairn to my north on the flank of another outrider, and thought to go there some other day and see what I might see. Barbon Fell has no summit to speak of. It has a trig point at what passes for its highest point, but otherwise it lies on the face of the earth like a fat sow of a mountain sleeping on its side; its back a Wastwater-like slope dropping steeply to the river, its head, legs, teats, and tail the ridges and outriders that fan out northwards to Lunesdale.

I saw a buzzard rise from the carcase of a sheep as I dropped from the heights and headed east for home, the late autumn sun now dropping towards Morecambe Bay and the sea lanes to Ireland. Fires coming on in the dale sent small plaits and curls of wood smoke into the still darkening air, and the first lights came on in houses along the dale as I dropped down towards my home.

Every step of my walk, from the moment I left the track past my house to the time I joined it again was a trespass, every boot-print broke the law. The CLA and the NFU would no doubt have me shot on sight. Yet who has the right to deny me (or any other human being on this planet) the right to walk in open uncultivated country on a day of wonder? Dante had a very low circle of Hell where he placed all the people he hated. In my lowest circle of Hell I would place, along with all the dictators, inventors of chemical and biological weapons, and other various despoilers of the world, all the be-grudgers and landowners who would keep us off the open moors and mountains; and if the Labour Party fail to deliver what they are bound to and what was in the hearts and souls of the people who gave the party its first blood, then I, like Dante, will consign them to a newly created lowest, sub-basement circle of Hell where they will be forced to look up the landowners bottoms.

December, 1997

Ramblers in Outer Space

According to the Ministry of Defence the number of walkers and climbers who claim to have seen extra terrestrial craft while out in the mountains has increased threefold in the last ten years. The ministry says, *'While some of these sightings can be put down to drink, hysteria, PMT, stray weather balloons, stealth bombers and missiles from Benbecula with wonky gimbals ending up over Crib Goch instead of St. Kilda, there still remains a sizeable file of reports from normal, sober, trustworthy people such as teachers, doctors and lawyers, that cannot easily be dismissed as hallucination or reflections from ice crystals in the sky.'*

Leaving aside the ridiculous idea that doctors, lawyers and teachers don't drink as much, and don't suffer from the same kinds of sensory blight as the rest of us lower grade humanoids, I was so intrigued that I decided to take matters further. I placed an advertisement in a national paper, asking for stories from people who had seen anything strange in the skies. This produced a body of evidence that convinces me that, not only have thousands of sightings been made in the hills of these islands, but that Close Encounters of the First Kind have been made on many occasions, particularly in areas where there are stone circles or alignments. It soon became obvious to me that such activity has always been strongest wherever there are ley-lines, hill figures or henges, pointing perhaps to the extra-terrestrial origin of much of the early religions of these islands. (As proposed in Erich Von Damart's classic *I Went Off in a Roman Catholic Flying Saucer*). A few examples from my notes and interviews may be of interest to readers.

Mr. C. J. (all names have been omitted to protect the privacy of the informant) of Cleckhuddersfax wrote thus:

'I teach law to doctors at Halifax University. I was walking with my wife and my dog near Stoodley Pike one cold October day. There was a clear blue sky, not a cloud in sight. Visibility was excellent, you could see all the way to Morecambe Clock Tower and Heysham Atom Plant. As we drew near the old stone circle at the top of Ballywarch Clough I noticed that something strange was happening. The dog refused to go any further. My wife and I were amazed. Then her hair stood up, she showed her teeth and nipped me; the dog began to behave strangely too. Then there was a *whooshing* sound and a flying saucer landed right in front of us. The sky suddenly went black and a door in the saucer's side opened to let down a ramp.

'It's that Jeremy Beadle,' said my wife.

'No I don't think it is,' I said. 'I think they're filming a Dulux advert. They have come to paint Stoodley Pike with that fluffy dog. It will be on the telly.'

'Then a creature came down the ramp holding one hand up in greeting, but when he got to the bottom of the ramp the dog ran up and bit him on one of his six legs and he scuttled back up, closed the door and the flying saucer flew off. Since then I have watched all the Beadle's About (except when I'm at Fretwork Class) and all the adverts but I have not seen anything of the one we were in. I can only assume it was an encounter with alien beings. My wife says it might have been street theatre like you see in the pedestrian precinct, and she has written to our local Tory MP. He wrote back to say he blames it on Calderdale Council being left wing. This wouldn't have happened under a Tory council he says, they wouldn't waste rate payers money on street theatre, but would spend it on Malayan dams and getting money for his mates in the construction industry instead.'

Another account came from Miss K. P. of Grimsby and details her more physical encounter with aliens. (It's interesting how many of the 'encounters' experienced by women seem to involve physical examinations of some kind). She writes:

'I'm a young lady doctor who specialises in treating sick law teachers. One clear, sunny, warm afternoon in high summer I was walking alone on Sgur Nan Pogmahone wearing nothing but boots and socks, a pair of shorts and a light tee-shirt. I was strolling along enjoying the peace and quiet when I heard a whooshing noise behind me. Turning round I saw a large flying saucer landing on the col. At first I thought it was perhaps a stunt organised by the Scottish Tourist Board, but then two green men climbed down a ladder and came towards me. I tried to run but something transfixed me. Strangely I felt very calm. They held up their hands and said something in their own language which of course I did not understand, but then one of them touched me with his scaly finger and immediately I could understand every word they said.

'Do not worry we will not harm you,' said one of the creatures. 'We only want to find out about you.' One of them took off my rucksack.

'Is it Berghaus?' his friend asked.

'No it's Karrimor,' the other replied.

'I wonder why so many of them use Karrimor?'

'It's because of that anatomical thingy. You know, the whatsit you can bend.'

'The colour's nice. I've always liked aubergine. It goes with my eye.'

'She's got a cagoule as well.'

'Well you never know in Scotland it can be shining one minute and all glackit and glooshy and coming down in stair rods the next.'

'And then there's the midges – they can be a right bugger.'

'Tell me about them. Is it Gortex?'

'Of course it is. You don't see much Ventile about nowadays.'

And then they just said, 'Thank you very much – have a nice day,' and climbed back in their space-craft and flew off again. I did notice that they'd pinched the Kendal Mint Cake from my rucksack.

March, 1995

Camels to the Pole

The other night, somebody in my local pub, The Yodelling Duck, gave me an ear bending about an article I wrote. 'Just daft it was,' he said. 'The magazine's all about adventure and exploration and danger and that, and your bit was just daft.'

I stared into my pint of Mother McCree's Milk of Amnesia and pondered. I haven't really had any adventures – much. I got chased by a dog once, but that was only exciting for a bit, and in any case it was only Jim Perrin's Jack Russell, and he did stop it biting me. I've never been in much danger either. There was a drunk who wanted to kill me once in a bar in Glasgow, but somebody took her home before she could do any damage. I once had a really bad headache that I thought might have been a brain tumour, but it was just a hangover, and that doesn't count as danger I suppose. As for exploration – well I've been to the bottom of K2 and Everest, and to the top of Kilimanjaro, and last year I went on a dog sledge across the ice cap in Greenland, but so have a lot of other people so that doesn't count as exploration. All in all I'm a bit of a washout when it comes to writing for an 'adventure' magazine – or whatever it's supposed to be called.

I stared into my now diminishing pint as glum as a bucket, a gloom descending about me like heavy cloud on the shoulders of Mt. Brandon. Then I had an idea. Years ago, in a dusty antiquarian book shop in Barnsley I had happened upon a bound sheaf of manuscripts and notebooks that had stirred my curiosity. Perhaps I could write about that?

It was a wet Wednesday afternoon, I was appearing as the juggler in *Aida* at the Barnsley Opera House, and there was an hour or two to spend between matinée and evening performance. I wandered down Shmecklegate, the old mediaeval heart of Barnsley, and noticed, between a ship's chandlers and the Oxthirst Shop a small, dust-encrusted window showing to the world a cluster of fly speckled tomes.

I opened the door, and somewhere far off a bell tinkled. All about me were piles of leather bound volumes: ancient hermetic treatise in Hebrew, cabalistic alchemical tracts, Fortesque's *Soup Collecting for Fun and Profit* and a rare volume of Spengler's *History of the East Dulwich Allotment Society* to 1893. I heard a shuffling noise behind me, and turned to see, coming towards me, an old man, grey haired and bent, wearing a snuff dusted, moth-gobbled cardigan, his twisted fingers peeping out of cut-down, knitted woollen gloves. He wore old carpet slippers on his feet, and had the snuff takers trademark: a dew drop nose. He coughed and a fog of old spilled snuff bloomed about him as a shaft of afternoon sunlight speared through the mirk of the cavernous book room. He looked me up and down for a moment.

'I think I know just what you're looking for,' he cackled, shuffling off.

What had this Magus read in my face? I asked myself. Had he discerned in my features a seeker after the truth, a lost soul wandering the earth looking for the answer to that great question – why are we here, of this tme, of this place? He shuffled back and thrust a volume towards me. It was a bound collection of *Health and Efficiency 1959-1963*.

'There's some good bits in that,' he winked. 'They've touched out the whatsits, but otherwise there's loads of fit bits with their kit off.' I handed it back to him in disgust.

'Haven't you got anything else? Climbing, walking, exploring – that kind of stuff?'

He cast his eyes to Heaven, then, pushing some wooden steps against the wall, climbed to the highest shelf, and brought down a dusty, oilskin covered bundle.

'One and six for the lot,' he grunted. 'Tek it or leave it. Rare manuscript. Never been seen before.' I paid him and left, and strangely, even though I have been back to Barnsley many times since, I've never been able to locate that strange shop, and when I ask people about it they look at me as though I'm mad.

'There's never bin a buck shop i'Barnsley lad. They stoned a bloke ter death 'ere in twenty six fer readin' bucks.'

Back in the dressing room, while the tenor was putting his slap on, and gargling with brandy and battery acid, I opened the bundle with shaking fingers. Inside was a collection of notebooks, diaries and papers. On the thickest notebook written in neat and precise stick-writing was, *Camels to the Pole – a true account of the first British Expedition to the Earth's Magnetic North Pole* – the author none other than Colonel Mungo Berghaus, the inventor of the Arctic jockstrap from which all modern rucksacks are descended. The journal told how Berghaus, reasoning that, if camel's feet stopped them sinking into the Saharan sands, then surely they would also be ideal in the thick snows of the Poles, bought a herd of camels from a Bedouin tribe in Eccles, Lancashire. He attempted to winterise them by leaving them for days in Pasagnio's Ice Cream Factory, Collyhurst. Some of the camels died of hypothermia, and customers had begun complaining that there was sand in their raspberry delights, so Berghaus abandoned that idea, and had special jackets and leggings knitted for them by Albemarles of Bond Street who had just kitted out the ill-fated Elphinstone Drinkpootle's expedition in search of the source of the River Irk.

Berghaus embarked aboard the *Golden Rivet* at Liverpool in 1871 and arrived in the Angmacapup Fjord in southern Greenland in the late spring, just as the ice in the sea lanes was melting .

I thumbed through the pages until I came to the entry for June 21st:

Jenkins expressed fears at dinner that we might be troubled by polar bears, and between us all it was decided to keep watches, naval style, during the hours of sleep. I took the dog watch, and it was during my watch that I discovered that though, our fears were real the bears were in fact not to cause us any great worry. I heard a noise and, looking up, saw through the clear midnight sun a group of polar bears approaching. Four or five in number they were mature and massive, and looked more than a little hungry. They began to circle the camp, then one of the leaders spotted the camels in their knitted jackets and leggings. He stopped dead in his tracks. I raised my Browning in case he made a charge but there was no need. He nudged the others and pointed towards the camels. The other bears stared in what I am sure was puzzlement. One of them began banging the side of his head with his paw as though to dislodge something. The others blinked and moaned to each other in a polar bear sort of way and looked totally baffled. Then, as one, they began what I can only describe as laughing. A chuckle spread through the group, then that became a laugh, that in its turn became a guffaw, and in no time at all the bears were rolling round in the snow hysterical with merriment. When they could stop laughing enough to stand, they turned and went back into the snowy vacuum from whence they came, shaking their heads and snorting with laughter.

I flicked the pages.

August the 22nd... Dear God but we are in a desperate way. We ate poor, dear Parkin's leg today, roasted over a fire made from what was left of the sledge, wrecked when the padre went berserk. We offered Parkin some; but he refused, saying he felt queasy and wasn't sure whether eating his own leg was not unchristian, so Smurfitt had his share and promised Parkin he shall have Smurfitt's snow ration. So you see in spite of everything we continue as English gentlemen. The Elsenham's Gentleman's Relish is all but gone. I do not know how much longer I can refrain from disclosing the news to the others.

So, though I cannot write of any great adventures myself, perhaps selected passages from the above might satisfy my tap-room detractor.

February, 1995.

Aliens are Stealing OUR Songs!

I sat in a pub in the Lakes the other day. I'd just come off the hill after a long day, and was in need of a little conversation with Frau Hopsundbarley. So there I was, sat with a glass in the midst of a dozen or more similar people with boots and cagoules and day sacks. The conversation was fairly lively, the evening sun was well over the yard-arm, and the pub was one of those few that has managed to escape being turned into a steak-house cum gift shop; but it suddenly struck me, as I sat there, that no-one was singing. I was on my own in the corner and am almost sure that if I'd started off with *The Manchester Rambler* or *Whisky in the Jar* somebody would have phoned for the men from the Funny Farm, and I'd have ended up swapping my Karrimor Baltoro for a straitjacket and a night in the hotel with the rubber walls.

As I sat there in that pub in the Lakes, I tried to remember – when was the last time that I heard a group of ramblers or climbers singing? Apart from last year when a load of us, snowed up while crossing Snow Lake in the Karakoram, tried to teach fifty Baltistani porters *Chick Chick Chick Chick Chicken Lay a Little Egg for Me*, it must have been three or four years ago in the Old Dungeon Gill in Langdale that I last heard a group of people having a good old lung clear out. What has happened? I ask myself. Am I wearing the rose-tinted goggles again, or were things really different a few years back? I know that many pub landlords now actually have signs up saying, *No Enjoying Yourselves by Order,* and that it's hard to find a publican nowadays who doesn't actually discourage smiling, and that pubs today are more retail outlets for multinationals to foist alcopops and fizzy lagers on us, but still and all, there must be some places where you can find a bit of *craic* at the end of a day out. I remain puzzled.

I've had hundreds of letters since the article about people being abducted by extra-terrestrials while out walking, and I am going to try and get round to answering them soon, but an interesting thing happened while I was on a walking holiday in New Mexico recently. I was mooching round a place called Roswell when I saw a sign above a small building proclaiming that it was *Roswell UFO Museum.* I went in, purely in the interests of research you understand, and asked a man behind the counter if he had any records of hikers being abducted while out walking. He produced a file a foot thick of incidents in New Mexico and Colorado, the most famous of which was the case of Griselda Marrowfat. She was hiking with a friend in the Sangre de Christos mountains near Taos, New Mexico, when a long silver object flew down and landed close by. It was the size of a small house. A door opened and a ramp was let down. Four little creatures in silver suits approached them.

Then something happened inside my head – Griselda writes – *I could understand every word they said to me.*

'Is this Crinkle Crags?' asked one of them, holding up a copy of a guide to the Lakeland Fells written by someone called Wainwright.

'No,' I said. 'You're about twenty miles from Taos, New Mexico.'

Immediately the one with the guide book hit one of the others on the head with it.

'You dozy prat!' he shouted. 'You told me you had your Pathfinder's badge! If we aren't back tonight the inter-stellar cave and fell rescue teams will be out looking for us.'

'He's always like this,' said one of the other aliens. 'Do you remember the last time? We climbed Ben Nevis and ticked it off on the Munro list, then we found out afterwards it was one of the pit heaps at Wigan, and those people down below weren't Scotsmen in kilts, just girls on their way to a Wigan Soul Night.'

'And another thing,' said one of the others, 'he never buys his round. He always manages to be last at the bar or in the toilet when it's his turn to get his feeler in his pouch!'

'All right!' said the one that had been hit. 'If you're all that clever you can organise the walks in future, because I'm fed up of being picked on. You don't realise how hard it is steering that thing with you lot singing and bawling in the back 'I've been a wild alien for many a year' and 'It's no nay never – ' and, 'I'm a rambler I'm a rambler from Betelgeuse way' – gets on me wick it does.'

Then they smacked him on the head a bit more before they all got back in the space ship and flew off.

Griselda's account was verified by her friend and two Mexican Jalapeno herders who were crossing the mountain at the time. Reading this first hand account it struck me that perhaps this was why there's no singing in the hiking pubs any more: the aliens have stolen all the songs. (I may be paranoid about this but remember even paranoids have enemies.)

I've had letters from people recently wanting to know more about 'Camels to the Pole' the account of the failed Mungo Karrimor expedition to the pole using Saharan camels wearing knitted jackets and leggings. One of the final entries in the journal reads:

Dear God, we must surely be close to the end by now. We ate the last of the camels this morning. We tossed for the hump and Parkin won it.

Simpson's feet are gone and Thompson's nose too. Poor Thompson, his glasses keep sliding down his face and falling off into the snow, but the dear fellow tries to make light of it. 'At least with no nose I won't have to smell your feet!' he said to Simpson this morning jocularly.

'What feet?' quipped Simpson. So you see, we still continue as English gentlemen.

June, 1995.

Landladies from Hell

One of the great mysteries of travel is the way that we are flung together, dumped, planted, dropped, and generally *fetched up* of necessity, in weird and sometimes wonderful habitations with assorted cohabitants, many of them the kind of people we would willingly consign over the side of the balloon basket in the game of the same name. I refer of course to the ubiquitous Bed and Breakfast.

In my years of travelling, walking and generally footling around various spots hot and otherwise in this world; sleeping in tents and lodges in the Himalaya, under the stars on St Kilda, and even in a bunkhouse on the floor of the Grand Canyon, I have never found anything on earth quite like the Great British and Irish Bed and Breakfast.

Some of them are wonderful, run by the kind of women you'd like to adopt as your mother; warm, clean, welcoming, making you feel that they value you as a traveller, and have some kind of respect for you. The best bed and breakfast in the world is The Credo in Killybegs, County Donegal, where, the last time I stayed there, breakfast was piles of Annie's scrambled eggs and smoked salmon with similar mountains of Frankie's home made soda-bread scones, and buckets of the kind of tea mice dream about trotting across. Three nights there would set you back roughly what one night in a cheap and nasty hotel in York would cost you.

But for every Credo there are of course the others, the Gulags of cold, damp, grubby unwelcoming pits with mad or bad landladies and landlords who were drummed out of the Gestapo for being too cruel. These places have nothing at all to recommend them other than that – like Life itself – the torment they deliver will ultimately come to an end.

How can I ever forget sitting wild eyed and delirious with lack of sleep as the major domo of one such establishment in the Highlands, a lay preacher with a badly fitting wig and a penchant for pastel cardigans, kept me up with his rendition of show tunes and popular melodies of the forties and fifties on a Bon Tempi organ, while his toothless aged and stinking poodle sat grinning gummily at me from its perch on the organ lid?

How can I ever forget the Adolphette Thatcher look-alike who ran the bed and breakfast on the North York Moors, and who made me change out of my walking boots in the car and wouldn't even let me take them off in the porch because they were muddy – that of course being the main function of walking boots – they get muddy so that your feet don't.

The same termagant lorded it over a house so full of chintz that, entering it was like going into a cave of Ercol, tie-backs, dralon and reproductions of bad paintings of squires sitting round inglenooks in coaching inns smoking clay pipes and being jocular with the barmaids. That was the only thing jocular in Casa Torycouncillorswife.

There were horse brasses everywhere: stuck to the imitation beams, ranged above the fireplace, as a frieze in the dining room, and following the rake of the stairs up the hall. I quite expected to find them sewn onto the corners of my pillow. And that brings me to the bed. I could never – for all the tea in China and India combined – be seen with a woman who wore white high heels with gold trimmings. Call me an old hippy if you like, but that's the way it is. Such shoes cry Tracy, Falaraki, and vodka and Red Bull to me, and I'm sorry but that's the way it is. I'm more a sandals, aromatherapy and Dingle Peninsula bloke. So it is with beds: the sight of a candlewick bedspread with massive roses on it on a bed with padded white plastic endboards with gold trimmings can drive me to the edge, and that night it did.

'Breakfast is between eight and nine, we like the rooms vacated by ten, we don't accept credit cards and I hope you're not a vegetarian,' she said flinging the door open with an operatic gesture, her massive bosom jiggling like a Portuguese Man of War that has just had its backside kicked. To compound the misery of the candlewick and the white plastic and gold, the sheets were nylon which meant that the slightest movement produced blue flashes of static that lit the darkness. I was glad I was on my own, any attempt at anything to do with fun would have generated enough electricity to light a small town. I slept badly, terrified in case I turned over too fast and set off a chain reaction that would set the alarms off at Fylingdales resulting in World War Two And A Half. Breakfast was cornflakes and pretend orange juice followed by dead stuff in setting grease, followed by white toast and the kind of marmalade that melts your fillings.

The worst bed and breakfast experience ever though was in a small and nasty Edwardian place called Duncarin on one of the south coast walking routes. It had everything Toryladyvillas had, including a landlady who had just had an operation for varicose veins. Now I don't find varicose veins funny – I don't suppose anybody does – but there I was, working my way through a very bad kipper that owed everything to the chemical industry and nothing at all to oak shavings, when in she came, plonked herself down in her house coat and slippers, lit up a fag and began to tell me about her operation.

Now I have a strong stomach. I have eaten all sorts of things in all kings of places: stinking shark in Iceland, goat's eyeballs in Oman, even the occasional Mcdonald's (Stafford, one Sunday in 1986 – everywhere else was closed) but, as I sat there with a bad kipper in front of me, she suddenly pulled up her housecoat to show me her scars. I forgot to mention that I had a champion hangover. The scars and sutures looked too like the spine and bones of my kipper for any kind of comfort and I was suddenly and spectacularly sick in one of the plant pots of geraniums on the windowsill – and I paid for the privilege.

August, 2002.

May Centipedes Inhabit Your Custard!

To paraphrase Donald Rumsfeld, AKA the Saviour of Democracy and Oil: *There are known knowns, there are unknown knowns, there are known unknowns, and there are unknown unknowns.* Ha Donald! I bite my thumb at you! May you be the father of budgerigars! May scorpions nest in your posing pouch! May Father Christmas and the tooth fairy forget where you live, and may the Angel of Death have an A to Z! Not only are you the murderer of many innocent Iraqis, you son of a piece of poodle poo, but you are also symptomatic of the great disease which has taken over all those in authority: the great knitted spectacles disease, by which I mean the pulling over the eyes of the wool (or attempts thereof) by the mangling of the language.

And they are all at it, particularly the BBC weather Peeps. Last week I stayed up late – well beyond yet another repeat of Frost – to catch the BBC weather forecast. The next day I planned to walk from Edale, climbing up Jacob's Ladder onto the rim of Kinder Scout, following the edge of the plateau as far as the day would let me. What with the days getting longer, and there being a promise in the offing of the sloughing of the thermal underwear, the little Harding heart was pit patting like a barefoot tapdancer on the hot plate of an Aga at the thought of getting out on Old Kinder, particularly since the Manchester to Sheffield train drops me off there, only about half an hour from the city centre, hence no driving at all.

'Frost,' said the man, pointing at a picture of a big owl flying towards a small witch, which turned out to be a chart of these strange little islands we live in.

'Just been watching it!' I shouted at the screen (once one is past a certain age one is allowed to dribble, pee one's pants and shout at the television).

Of course it was not David Jason he was talking about, but the white, crispy stuff.

'Frost inland and in exposed places will be followed by a clear sunny day across most of the British Isles.' He went on to say that everything in the garden was triple tickety and double boo, and that we would probably all be getting sunstroke if we didn't watch out. Beware false prophets.

Next morning, light of heart and heavy of rucksack, I got off the train at Edale and set off for the Scout. There was a lot of cloud about, and no frost at all to be seen, but the BBC is a venerable organ, known and respected the world over, so who was I to doubt their weatherman? As I plodded upwards, all on my Jack Jones and not another soul to be seen, the drizzle began to fall. Then, deciding that it was fed up being drizzle, it turned into proper rain. It went on this way for a bit longer, then (with the attention span of a nine year old Sony Game Boy Fan in a reference library) it decided it was fed up being rain, and wanted to be a sleety downpour. *The BBC can't be wrong,* I thought, scrambling up what had once been a path, and was now a minor mountain torrent, *Any minute now the sun will come cracking out, steam will rise from the peat bogs, and my nose will start to peel.*

Gentle reader, it did not. In the spirit of known unknowns and unknown knowns the man with the clicker and the pretty chart at Broadcasting House had been talking meteorological gonads via his fundament. The rain became lashing hail for a while, then settled back to just being heavy rain. After a couple of hours of masochistic bog trotting I ate my sarnies, and drank my tea in the lee of some big rocks that had not been there when I was a lad, and decided to call it a day.

Later, on the warm train back to the metropolis, I remembered another day when the BBC had almost killed me. In our B and B in Grasmere, at roughly the same time of the year I had watched a handsome young weatherman who shall be nameless, called Francis, explain that the next day was going to be all sunshine and blue skies, particularly in the North of England.

The next morning, our rucksacks filled with confidence and packed lunches we set off for Coniston Old Man. I have a photograph of me at the highest point we got to that day. Somewhere well below the summit I am standing, barely visible, in a white-out, ankle deep in freshly fallen snow. We got off the hill mainly because the lady I was with could use a map and compass, hadn't panicked, and wasn't calling for her mummy, as I was. It took a lot of glasses of single malt and a bowl of cockie leakie before I felt strong enough to face the world after that little jaunt.

As it happened, the next week I was appearing on the BBC breakfast show – the one hosted by Frank Bough – I forget the name of it (once one is past a certain age one is allowed to dribble, pee one's pants and forget stuff).

There on set was the same weatherman, handsome, gifted and wrong. When he had finished his bit of clicking and fibbing, and while he was still on set, and we were still on air, I asked Frank Bough if I could show him (and the watching nation) last Wednesday's weather on Coniston Old Man.

The camera zoomed in on the photograph of me in the white-out, I repeated the forecast for that day, and a purple faced, handsome and wrong weatherman said, 'You should have taken account of the local conditions.'

Was this a known known, or an unknown unknown? Why bother at all if you don't pigging well know! Tish push you weather people. I bite my tongue at you! May you be the fathers and mothers of politicians! May centipedes inhabit your custard! May pigs roost in your airing cupboards, and may the bluebird of happiness miss your door, and instead may the crow of misery poo in your chilled Chardonnay! (Once one is past a certain age one is allowed to dribble, pee one's pants and curse people).

March, 2005.

Fixing Broken Teeth in Namche Bazaar

You sound just like Chas and Dave said the American lady with the five thousand dollar teeth and the bosom like the fender of a Ship Canal tug.

Coming into Newman's pub in Geggan, Connemara, after a long day on the hill, and finding the session in good form, I had been asked to, *give us an old strain or the bar or two of a ditty, anything at all you understand, take your time there's no hurry.*

I find it difficult to sing Irish songs in a Manchester accent when I'm in the west of Ireland, so I sang a cod country and western song about a man who is in love with a sheep, and who is lamenting both her absence and the long prison sentence he has been given for carrying on such a dubious relationship. Animal husbandry, to give it its incorrect title, is not unknown in certain areas of this planet I believe, though, like incest and voting Conservative, it is something I'm not terribly interested in. In fact I don't know anybody who has had a sheep or chicken for a girlfriend, though George Melly, the jazz singer, claims that something of this ilk did in fact happen while he was in the merchant navy in the nineteen fifties, when one of his fellow sailors was arrested for having carnal knowledge of a sheep. In court the defendant claimed that owing to his bad eyesight he had mistaken the sheep for a WREN in a duffel coat. I can't remember now whether he got off – the charge I mean. However I digress.

The cod country and western song what I wrote is called, *Dancing Alone in the Night,* has a chorus of bleats and baas, and would no doubt have Garth Brooks spinning in his grave were he not still alive. But it was then, when the Bostonian dowager likened me to two chirpy pearly kings, that it occurred to me what unlikely bed fellows travel makes of us all. We world travellers, walkers, climbers, ramblers – be it whatever we be – are flung from time to time into remote corners of the globe where we rub shoulders and cross swords with other lumps of jetsam and flotsam, thankfully usually only for the duration.

I mean Chas and Dave! Much as I like the lads, only an American could mistake an accent tempered by gritstone and Viking axes, Hardcastle Crags and Kinder Scout for one that extols the virtues of jellied eels, people covered in pearl buttons and the Kray Brothers! I didn't disabuse the American lady since to do so would have been both tedious and embarrassing, and probably lengthy – since all Americans imagine that everybody from England sounds like Dick Van Dyke, while everybody from Ireland sounds like Darby O'Gill. Americans are strange; nice but strange.

I once, for no reason which would interest you now, found myself sitting on a wall in a small town where the Appalachian Trail wandered across the black top. A lady started talking to me then, hearing my accent, asked me where I was from. 'England,' I answered.

She smiled and said, 'England! How nice! I have some friends went on vacation to a village in England once called Italy.' I swear on my scout woggle that the story is absolutely true. And this was at the height of the Cold War when American nuclear warheads were targeted on any Russian city with more than two people in it. If they thought Italy was a village in England, where the hell did they think Moscow was? In Milton Keynes? Behind the Dog and Trumpet pub in Bingley? Down the settee with the remote control? Travel does surely make strange bedfellows of us all.

I remember once climbing Kilimanjaro with a Harley Street gynaecologist who snored for England. What I was doing in the snows of that equatorial dud volcano is not germane to the tale, his snoring is. His snoring was of Olympic standards, and was less a snore than a catalogue of sound effects. As I lay asleep in the bunkhouse under the snow line during a long sleepless African night I heard, in random order, and repeated throughout that long, long night; three ducks arguing in Greek in a wet cardboard box, followed by two wart hogs mating in a swimming pool full of warm tapioca pudding. This in its turn was followed by an impression of Louis Armstrong scat singing with a mouth full of cinder toffee while kick starting an old moped underwater.

I remember vividly how a French lady climber in her sixties, who had been sleeping on the floor of the hut in a survival blanket, suddenly stood up, still wrapped in her silver blanket and screamed at him, 'Monsieur!! You snore!! You snore!!' which is a bit like telling the sea that it is wet.

'Yes I do, and I do it very well too,' said the gynaecologist before falling back into another raucous and mega-decibeled stupor. Lit by the African moon the scene looked rather as though the ladies' bits inspector was being attacked by a giant Gallic talking sausage wrapped in Bacofoil, and it struck me then, as a lapsed Catholic of no fixed abode, that if I'd had any sense and had done what my mother told me and got a nice job as an accountant and had married Dierdre O'Halloran and settled down, I wouldn't have been there in that hut with these two nutters in the first place.

Strange bedfellows. A few years before while nursing my blisters at Namche Bazaar on the way up to Everest Base Camp I met up with a group of American trekkers on the way down.

'You guys got any news?' one of them shouted across the crowded tea lodge. I had heard from somebody back home that both the London Stock Exchange and Wall Street had suffered a cataclysmic melt down that had wiped trillions off the price of shares – I think they called it Black Wednesday or Green Friday or Yellow Tuesday or something (what do I know about economics anyway? I'm a banjo player.)

'Yes,' I said, 'Wall Street has just gone down the pan, and the Dow Jones has gone from eight zillion and sixpence to tuppence farthing on the Beaufort Scale (it was something like that anyway, I had the figures in my head at the time but like I said, I'm a banjo player.)

The man who had asked the question staggered back clutching his chest in the first throes of a heart attack.

'Where can I get to a fax machine?' he shrieked. Now in Namche you can get very nice apple pie and yak steak, you can buy some Buddhist finger bells if you want, and even a pair of very good second hand Koflachs left behind by some expedition or other, but in them there days – fax machines? Not.

Somebody sat on the guy's head, and somebody else applied burning yak dung to his bare feet in a vain attempt to calm him down. It was no use. He was inconsolable. He was an orthodontist from L.A. who, after amassing fortunes making everybody's teeth look like white corn on the cob, had taken early retirement and sunk every penny of his loot in the stock market. He would now have to go back home and start fitting more bits of wire into people's gobs to make them all look the same. Had there been a daily paper in Namche, such as the Namche Bugle, it would have had as its headlines, *Yankee Toothdoctor Loses Trousers In Wall Street Crash.* Strange bedfellows – you bet.

November 1999

Bin Laden Crunchy Bar

I was in America recently in Virgina, visiting family and taking the odd day out to ramble along sneaky bits of the Appalachian Trail. I've walked patches of the Trail before, mostly in North Carolina and I did once cycle the roads that run parallel to the trail for a BBC series, but I have to tell you that, dans mon humble opinion, it's quite a boring walk and far too long. Before I get swamped with angry letters from Vermont and California let me say that there are some great stretches of the route when the land opens out, and you get to see something, and there are some very tough bits of the route, so it's not a walk for softies, but somehow spending six months or more of your life walking forest trails isn't my idea of fun, particularly since, unlike the Pennine Way there are lots of things that will try to kill you such as bears, rattle snakes and the occasional loony. You also stand a very strong chance of being lampooned in one of Bill Bryson's travel books.

It was during one of my excursions into the Appalachians a few years back that I was fed rattlesnake in a chilli. Rattlesnake was a new taste to me, it doesn't figure in the chip shops of Yorkshire or in the curry shops of Curry Mile where I am wont to fill my pouch from time to time. Harry Ramsden's as far as I know has yet to offer *Rattler, Chips, Mushy Peas, Tea, Bread and Butter* on its Specials board and I know for certain that the Chittagong Indian Restaurant in Salford does not offer Tandoori Rattlesnake Marsala. However I digress. The gentleman who served the dish was a third generation Scot who wore a kilt and a stetson, played the bagpipes and blues harmonica, and had the rattle and the skin from our dinner fastened round his ten gallon. After the meal, which was accompanied by tins of McEwan's Export and shots of Mountain Dew, we had games, one of which, a pea-pushing competition, I won by pushing a dried pea along a piece of rush matting, some ten feet or so in length, with my nose. The woman who came second was my host's wife, an actress of no mean ability who played the woman who shot her husband in *Midnight In The Garden Of Good and Evil.* She was so determined to beat me that she became terribly erratic in her pushing and gave herself quite bad friction burns to the tip of her nose. Luckily she wasn't appearing in any films that week because she ended up with a nasty little scab on the end of her retroussé little bogie box. So I suppose you could say that the Appalachian Trail might be boring but the people you meet along the way ain't.

I ended up in Leesburg somewhere along the way and wandered into a shop in search of stuff (America is very good on stuff – they have more of it than anywhere else on the planet) and the lady who sold the stuff engaged me in a small bit of banter.

'Where y'all from?' she asked. 'I do like your accent.'

I decided to be obtuse and said, 'I was born in Lancashire but I live most of the time in Connemara now with occasional sojourns in Manchester.'

'Well really!!' she exclaimed. 'Mah husband and I go Morris Dancing, and we do that Lancashire Morris, you know the one where you use the clogs. But we cain't find a clog-maker in Virginia no more. The last one finished three years ago. Wait 'till ah tell mah husband ah've met somebody from Lancashire.'

As I made my way back into the woods I couldn't help but wonder if there was group of people in Todmorden or Burnley who at that very moment were dancing Appalachian style in tap shoes and dirndl skirts to the sound of fiddle and frailing banjo? I suppose I'll never know.

Keeping supplied along the Appalachian Trail (certainly on the sections I've walked) has hardly been a problem since there are outfitting shops in most of the small towns and villages along the route that sell everything from Indian canoes, backpacks, boots and tents, to trail food. Amongst the trail food I came across on this trip in the Blue Ridge Mountains was *The Bible Bar.*

A devout Christian called Tom Ciola who has spent thirty years in the sports nutrition game has invented an energy bar that contains the seven foods mentioned in Deuteronomy: wheat, barley, raisins, honey, figs, pomegranates and olive oil. He is also the inventor of a breakfast cereal called *Bible Granola,* an energy bar called *The Seeds of Samson,* and something called *Back To The Garden – a Bible Based Meal Replacer.* Mr Ciola (and I swear every word of this is true) has also written a self-help diet guide called, *Moses Wasn't Fat.* Well after all those years wandering round lost in the desert, dividing seas and turning sticks into snakes (before eating them in chilli one assumes) he would hardly be chubby would he?

Munching on the *Bible Bar,* as I made my way through the woods towards some more woods, I wondered whether there could be a trail food for Atheists? Then I decided that an energy bar called *There's Nothing There* or, *It's All A Load Of Rubbish* would hardly be best sellers. Agnostics might fare better with stuff like *The Perhaps Pecan Bar* or *Doubters Doughnuts.* But still none of that stuff quite has the ring of *The Bible Bar,* and I can just imagine George Bush munching on a *Seeds Of Samson* as he wobbles round the White House sticking pins in maps of places his tiny mind has no understanding of, but feels he should bomb anyway. Perhaps the other lot could come up with something – *Taliban Tucker? Al Qaeda Sport Drink? A Bin Laden Crunch Bar* anybody?

February, 2003.

Mick's Magic Potato

I was eating a potato the other day when I was suddenly, mid-bite, transported to Zanskar in Northern India. I was in Ireland when it happened, making dinner in the cottage in Connemara which made it all doubly strange. It wasn't that my potato had become magical like Jimmy's Magic Patch. (For those not old enough to remember, Jimmy was a small boy in a comic in the fifties – I think it was *The Wizard* – who had a patch sewn into his trousers. Little did he know that the patch came from an old magic carpet, so that whenever he rubbed the patch he was whizzed off across the world.)

No, gentle reader, it was no magic potato, simply a humble spud from the local market. It was the texture and taste of the spud that took me back to Zanskar; it was the twin brother or sister of the potatoes we were given by our cookboy on the very first trek I did in the Himachal Pradesh way back in the mists of whatsit. We were trekking from Darcha to Padum across the Shingo La with a pony man, a cookboy and a half dozen ponies. It was my first trip to the Himalayas, and the sights, colours and smells of that journey into the high mountains are still etched deeply into my memory. Strange that a potato can take you back there – and much cheaper than a BA flight to Delhi.

I'd managed to get some organic potatoes at Clifden market and when I put them on the plate and cut into them the world shifted slightly, and my mind went back to that first day years ago when we paused in our first day's march, and opened the bag to see what cookie had given us for lunch stop. Wrapped in greaseproof paper were a hard-boiled egg, two chapatis folded and smeared with jam, a couple of apples, some boiled sweets, two boiled potatoes and a twist of salt in paper. It doesn't sound much, but I suspect that a dietician might find it a reasonable meal for a day's trek: some protein, plenty of carbohydrate and some fruit. Whatever the dieticians think, it went down well, particularly the cold potatoes. They were waxy and firm and tasted like potatoes should. So did those in Ireland. Whether they were the same strain I wouldn't know. According to a guy I met in Pokhara the potato made its way into the Himalayas with returning British Army Gurkhas, and in some places took over from barley as a staple crop. So that's probably why, at Namche Bazaar on the Everest walk in, you can get a plate of very good chips to go with your yak steak.

Which reminds me – the first time I went to Namche Bazaar was by helicopter. I was making a film for Channel Four on the pollution all along the trail to Everest Base Camp caused by mass tourism. In those days much of the trail was quite filthy: discarded cans and bottles, cartons, human excrement, and yards and yards of pink toilet paper littered the sides of the path. The film was called *The Kleenex Trail – Everest The Soft Way*, and did a little (I like to think) to help the problem, because many years later, leading a trek for Karakoram Experience, I saw that the way was as clean as you would want: the lodges we stayed at (we camped) were spotless, the toilets perfect, and the trail itself pretty much clear of western rubbish. I haven't the time here to go into arguments vis-à-vis mass tourism versus local cultures so let's leave that aside for the moment – this is about food.

On my first night in Namche I was alone, waiting for the film crew and my producer to arrive from back down the trail. The cloud rolled in dead on time at four o'clock, as it does in Namche post monsoon. It was cold and dismal, and it was my birthday, the twenty third of October and the first of three birthdays I've spent in Nepal. I happened to mention this to an American guy who was sitting in the lodge with me, and two minutes later he came back into the dining room with a huge slice of chocolate cake with a candle stuck in it singing Happy Birthday. At the same time the cassette player in the dining room started playing Ralph McTell singing *Streets of London.* Only weeks before Ralph and I had been on the same team of 'celebrity' cricketers getting hammered by the local cricket team at a fund-raising match in Jake Thakeray's old village in Monmouthshire. So there I was on my birthday in the mists of Namche Bazaar eating chocolate cake while listening to Ralph's best tonsil work. I was well impressed and to this day I can't hear *Streets of London* without thinking about Namche Bazaar and chocolate cake.

The chocolate cake by the way, like the potato and the wonderful apple pies you can get further down the valley, is largely due to returning Gurkhas bringing recipes back from the British Army Messes. That night I also dined on yak steak and chips. The chips were delicious, if small, and were made with the spuds that came from terraced fields that had already been flattened to take the next crop: trekkers' tents. The yak steak however was another kettle of fish entirely. Imagine eating a draught excluder that has been soaked in chilli sauce, and you might just get some idea. Yaks are aggressive and unpredictable creatures and their meat is just the same. To this day I can't look at a draught excluder without thinking of yak steaks and that night in Namche Bazaar.

Strange to think that the potatoes I had in Zanskar and Nepal came from a stock introduced from Britain, and that Britain itself only got the plant when Sir Walter Raleigh brought it back from America, and tried to get Good Queen Bess to smoke one. What a curious world we live in where a potato can take you across the world.

October, 2005.

A Loaf of Bread, a Glass of Wine, some Calamari Mousse?

I was in my local outdoors shop the other day and, amongst all the GPS stuff and other new fangled gizmos (such as, in no particular order: inflatable gas stoves, spray on tents, and packs of dehydrated water) was a load of freeze-dried gourmet meals designed by one of the more famous TV chefs. Now I don't want to upset anyone, but to get me to watch a TV cooking show such as, *Ready Steady Fricassée* or *Can't Poach, Won't Poach,* you'd have to pry my eyelids open with that thingy they put on Malcolm McDowell in *Clockwork Orange.* It has always seemed to me that those programmes (and those bloody gardening shows – and those pigging house decorating shows – now I'm on about it) are to Television what Herod is to Babies R' Us. However I digress.

What I wanted to say is that the freeze dried meals in the shop were not such normal type stuff as, Irish Stew, Spanish Omelette or Chicken Curry: they were *Beef Napoleon With Passion Fruit Sauce, Calamari Mousse* and *Fruite de Mure Compote with Gooseberry and Greek Brandy Coulis*, and *Wild Boar and Salmon en Croute with a Chocolate Gooseberry Dip.* Now call me old fashioned but, when I were a lad, we'd go all day on a bowl of porridge and a dripping butty, and our meal, when we made camp at night full of blisters, sunburn and nettle stings, would be sausage and beans and a mug of cocoa. I still believe that nothing beats the smell of bacon frying on a wood fire while the dew is yet upon the grass, not even my first sniff of *Evening In Paris* on the neck of Bernadette Lakeland, St Anne's RC School, Crumpsall, Manchester, circa 1957. As Omar Khayyam once wrote in his *Boys' Own Rubaiyat*:

O come with Old Khayyam and leave the rest
To eat their freeze dried junk; give me
A rasher of bacon, sausage, beans, two eggs
And thou beside me wafting hot sparks up me legs,

How true.

And yet, with the ice caps melting, and sperm no longer being able to count, we eschew the noble spud and the humble banger of our rambling ancestors for a freeze dried, artificial paradise conjured up by some overweight lunatic in checked trousers and a pinny, with a mansion in Dorking, a villa in Torremolinos, a five hundred pound a week cocaine habit, a Rolls Royce campervan, and a wife with botox lips and silicone buttocks who's had so many face lifts her navel is now on her chin. Baden Powell would be turning in his grave if he hadn't been cremated.

What is it with people nowadays? When I were a lad we'd walk all day sucking pebbles like Baden Powell taught you to, with a big spud in our pockets to roast in the hot ashes of the campfire while we sat round singing *Oh My Darlin' Clementine* and the song *Gin Gan Gooly*. Kids of today!!!

And another thing: as any SAS trooper will tell you, eating that kind of tucker is what lost the Americans the Vietnam War. They ate all that processed junk: freeze-dried cheeseburgers and fries (just add water) and freeze-dried coke (just add water) then they sat down and smoked a camel or two. (Why did the RSPCA do nothing about this one wonders?)

Then they would go in the jungle, and their sweat would smell of cheeseburgers, and their breath would smell of camels, and the Viet Cong (all of whom were called Charlie by the way) would smell them coming miles away and would lie in wait wearing nothing but rubber tyres and then would kill them all. The SAS on the other hand (and they were out there no matter what the government says) used to eat what Charlie did: stones and water buffalo poo – and what was the casualty rate amongst the SAS in the jungles of Vietnam? I rest my case.

I went on a camping trip a year or so back, wild camping on the tops in the Dales. I'm sure I was breaking all sorts of laws; but at least I wasn't churning up the country on a trials bike. I took hardly anything in the way of food, preferring instead to live off the land. But after two days of eating peat I went into Malham and bought six packs of dried soup. Unfortunately, that night on top of Shunner Fell there was no water so I chewed the soup dry. Still you mustn't complain. And, talking about complaining, here's a true story.

There's a pub in Giggleswick called the Hart's Head to which I am known to repair on the odd occasion (i.e. when the month has a vowel in it, or when oyster has an 'r' in it.)

The landlord is a bit of a wag and, one night, for a nobble, I called him over and said, 'If this was a proper pub, at the end of the night we'd all get a slice of bread and dripping free and gratis. Malcolm at the Helwith Bridge always used to give his customers bread and dripping at this time of the night.'

This is in fact true, as any historian with a working knowledge of the pubs of the Yorkshire Dales will tell you: at closing time Malcolm, the landlord of The Helwith Bridge would put on a bowler hat, sing Methodist hymns, and pass round a tray of delicious beef dripping on toast as a pet lamb wearing a nappy walked round the pub bleating.

A few moments later Trevor the landlord of the Harts Head came out of the kitchen, and handed me a slice of bread. It was bread and dripping all right – it was bread dripping – he'd run it under the tap. Laugh! I thought I'd never start.

And if you believe nothing else in this page of lunacy, the latter is one hundred and five per cent true.

February, 2005.

First Harp on Everest

I met a bloke in a pub the other day who told me he'd just finished the last of the Munros, and now he was looking for another challenge. Now I don't want to sound like a curmudgeonly nang but I'm not sure about Munro bagging, it seems like a more energetic form of train spotting, the kind of thing you wouldn't be surprised to find John Major doing: wandering the fells with his little bobble hat on, ticking them all off in his Winnie the Pooh notebook. I don't know, maybe I'm weird, but I go to the hills for the peace and the solitude and the grandeur of the world, not to collect them like thimbles or Lilliput Lane cottages. Still, to each his own I suppose and it's better than collecting guns.

I suggested to the ex-Munro bagger that he could try doing them all again backwards or blindfolded, or he could spin plates on the top of them all, or try and make love on the summit of every three thousand footer, only not on bank holidays, or some Brown Owl is going to have a lot of explaining to do. He didn't seem very impressed. I thought the making love idea was quite good, and suggested it to the long haired side of the household. It was greeted with first an incredulous look then a laugh and, 'Don't tell me you've forgotten what happened on Whernside that hot Thursday in 1986! "There's nobody round for miles," you said and the next minute fourteen twitchers were all round us looking for the nest of an Arctic Hummingbird or something. It's a good job I didn't take you up on your suggestion.'

People have done funny things up mountains. Having your ashes scattered on your favourite mountain is becoming increasingly popular. Leaving aside the planning aspects of such activities (covered in the 1966 legislation on erection of chicken houses, widening of lay byes and disposal of mortal remains in National

Parks and SSSIs) I'm not sure if it isn't perhaps a little ghoulish. If you get a piece of dirt or grit in your eye on a mountain summit now you'll never know whether it's a piece of genuine granite dust or a bit of the carbonated tibia of Tom Smith of Doncaster, husband, father and general good sort who loved these hills and was scattered here last week. If human cinder dumping goes on much longer they reckon that Suilven will be only eleven metres lower than Everest. Well that will make the Scottish Tourist Board happy, and perhaps take their mind off the midges.

Craziest thing I ever heard was a woman who tried to get a harp up Everest. She was seen going through Namche Bazaar a few years back, a porter struggling along behind her carrying a full size concert harp while she strode on wearing a tee-shirt that proclaimed, *First Harp On Everest.* I rather hoped that she would fall off and could just imagine St Peter at the gates watching her approach, 'Here Boss, cop for this one, she's only gone and brought her own bloody harp with her!'

I have to admit that I did create an imaginary pub once on top of a mountain. Not to get myself up, it was to motivate a pal of mine called Big Phil enough to get him to the top of Pen y Ghent. Phil was, and still is, a big lad, a diet of five pounds of spuds in the chip pan together with teens of pints of ale combined to make him Lancashire's only non-wrestling sumo. He's actually quite a keen walker and used to go on long walks with another pal, Tex. They used to get the train out of Manchester to a station somewhere in the hills like Hebden Bridge or Edale, walk fifteen miles or so over the fells to another station and get the train home. They were both however partial to a pint or two and the *craic*, and often they went the way of all flesh, and fell amongst thieves. One such day they got to a pub at Heckmondwyke around opening time, having walked all of a mile and half from the station at Hebden Bridge, and stayed there all day. As the landlord swept up about them that night he looked into what was left of their eyes and asked, "How many miles do you do to the gallon lads?"

But back to the story. On this particular hot August day I told

Phil that there was a bar on the summit of Pen y Ghent run by the local cave rescue team in aid of funds, and that it served pints of ice-cold Theakstone's bitter and ploughman's lunches.

'How do they get it all the way up here?' he gasped.

'They use a donkey,' I lied.

'A donkey couldn't climb that!' he said, stopping and looking up at the gritstone scramble up The Neb.

'They bring it up the other side, it's easier.'

'Must be a tough rascal donkey that!'

We borrowed a walking stick from an octogenarian who was climbing the hill on his birthday to get Phil up the final hard pull while I ran over the top, past the trig point, and off down the hill. Now Phil has one of the best swearing vocabularies I have ever heard and I could hear his cursing even when I was at Hull Pot. He scandalised several dozen people that day, and it was all my fault. He forgave me that night in the Helwith Bridge but only after a few pints of Tetley's had taken away the pain in his knees. He never was one to harbour grudges.

Reading this article back it seems to me to be all about sex and alcohol and not at all the kind of earnest, searching, well considered and polished prose piece the editor asked for. Well, sometimes Life is like that, and I promise to do better next time. Honest.

January, 1995

Cheers Uncle Bobby

I was born in a small red brick terraced house in a place called Crumpsall, Manchester. A lot of people don't believe that Crumpsall exists, but that it's like Narnia in the C. S. Lewis books, and the only way you can get there is through the back of a wardrobe. When I do poetry readings and slide shows I describe Crumpsall as *a picturesque spa fishing village,* in most places the line gets a laugh though, more than once I've been asked if there are any nice hotels there where people can go on holiday.

Crumpsall, at least the part I lived in, was dominated by the C.W.S. Cream Cracker factory, a brake lining works, and the biggest dye and chemical complex in Europe. The biscuit factory gave off a sweet sometimes sickly smell, the brake lining factory gave out a baked asbestos smell, and the dye factory gave out a stench that ranged from straight chemical fug to something Dante would have put in the bowels of Hell. On hot summer days the baking streets could sometimes be deadly – nausea, streaming eyes, bronchitis, asthma – we had a preview of the death of the ozone layer forty years ago. Ranged about were more factories and mills and, closer in towards the city, iron and steel works, a rubber stick-on-sole factory and a glue factory that employed what was then called 'the sub-normal' at below living rates to boil the bones and carcasses down.

A railway line runs through Crumpsall. It is now part of the Metro tram service. Then it was the electrified Manchester to Bury line, and to me as a kid in the streets of that picturesque spa fishing village, it was an escape route. From the age of seven until my early teen years I would spend every holiday I could in what I then thought was 'the country' a small suburb on the edge of the last park land and open country north of Manchester called Besses o' th' Barn. We go in for names like that in the north. The whole place was named after a hostelry that served the pack men and the waggoners travelling north to Bury and Bolton, the pub was run by a woman called Bessy and it had once been a barn so the story goes. To me Besses was 'the country' and I went there to 'have adventures'.

My Uncle Bobby and Aunty Kitty lived in Besses, and they would have me up to stay with them for weeks at a time, and nobody knew happier times than I had then. Uncle Bobby was a socialist when that was not a dirty word. He believed in the essential goodness of Man, and believed that it was only ignorance and fear that allowed the powerful and the mad to dominate and destroy the rest of us. Forty years on I can find nothing to counter that argument. Uncle Bobby McGloughlin was of immigrant Irish stock, a tailor from the Strangeways area of the city who had somehow managed to move out to Besses, to a tiny house on the edge of the old park land of the Phillip's Estate. He would take me walking with him and Vic his black Labrador dog, through the cloughs and the fields of that last of the green land. We would walk all day by streams and over meadows. Vic would chase a hedgehog, and end up with holes in his nose, I would see wild flowers and birds that wouldn't have lasted ten minutes in the industrial soup of the city air.

When Bobby was working I'd go alone down the Clough, following the stream under the high, brick-built bridge spanning the gorge that the Phillips had built to ride their horse-drawn carriages to the great hall. I followed that stream for miles to a great mill pool, lodges we called them in Lancashire, where fishermen nodded over slack lines in the hot sun. Other days Bobby and I would get on the bus and travel beyond Besses to the moors above Bury. We'd walk and talk until the sun dropped low against the heather, and it was time to head home again. The great thing about walking with Uncle Bobby was that he didn't see children as idiots. He talked to me as though I was a sort of grown up with a limited vocabulary, if you see what I mean, bright enough to understand most ideas, if they are put in the right way.

As I grew older I joined the Boy Scouts and went away to camp in exotic places like Devon and Kent. Later still I went hiking and climbing with spotty youths who like myself were just starting to shave, drink, and realise that girls aren't just boys who can't climb trees without showing their knickers.

Why am I telling you all this? I suppose I'm trying to understand something of my own past, to understand how the love of the open spaces that Uncle Bobby fostered in me ran through me, and still runs through me like a hunger. I'm sure that it is because of him that I've spent so many of the last twenty years walking in places as far apart as Littleborough and Ladakh. But I think that perhaps I'm telling you this also because I have just met Uncle Bobby again after twenty odd years. He's ninety five now living with his daughters in Toronto, still as left wing as ever, brews his own beer, and is a rabid ice-hockey fan. We talked for hours about places we'd been together on those long hot days of summer. I hadn't the heart to tell him that the M62 has ripped its way through the heart of that magical clough where we wandered, or that multi-screen cinema complexes, supermarkets and do-it-yourself mega stores now cover most of that lovely meadow land, or that estates of red brick 'Executive Homes' are marching up the flanks of many of those lovely Pennine valleys where we roamed. It was better that we stuck to remembering the good times.

Flying back on the plane later that week another thing struck me – that if this was anything like a proper world, every kid in it would have an Uncle Bobby.

August, 1998

Munchkins in Gortex

I set off from the back of the house the other day to climb up onto the scar that looms up dark and craggy behind us, challenging me every morning, reminding me that it is several days since I had my boots on, and reminding me how, when I lived in Manchester all the time, I was on the hills every weekend as though it was an addiction, and, now that I live in the middle of them I get out half as much. So, I shut down the computer, threw on my boots and jacket and set off.

Half way up the crag I felt a sudden chill draught wafting its way round the bits that even Heineken doesn't get to. I felt around gingerly in the general region of the blast, and discovered that a long stretch I had made while scrambling over a drystone wall, had split my pants from apex to breakfast. I was a bit annoyed because they were a favourite pair of walking trousers, and this meant that, since I'd already repaired them a good few times, they would next be seen in public on the kids' Guy Fawkes. It also meant that I would have to buy another pair, and if there is anything I hate more than buying clothes it is buying more clothes. It's not that I'm mean, I'm not. It's just that when you're my shape and size everything you put on looks as though you're wearing it for a bet.

Norfolk Intrepid Hats for instance. Norfolk Intrepid Hats are really good outdoor hats that can be found advertised in the back of various of the Sunday papers on the page with the Tanga Thongs, latex bedsheets and other 'exciting adult pleasure products.' If you're shaped like Crocodile Dundee or Harrison Ford, Norfolk Intrepid Hats look great on you. If you're more like a cross between Charley Drake and a Munchkin then they do you no favours at all. You look like a cowboy that's fallen into one of those machines they have in scrapyards that turn cars into small metal cubes, or even worse, a character from Snow White and the Seven Vertically Challenged Gauchos.

Trousers are another thing. (I don't mean this to be exclusively male by the way, I'm sure women suffer from similar problems it's just that, not having yet entered my cross-dressing stage, most of my experiences are to do with men's stuff.) Most men's trousers are made for 'normal' people which seems to mean round about five feet nine and a quarter. I always have that much extra leg flapping about beyond my toes that I could make a fair sized draught excluder, or enough tubular overcoats for a pair of dachschunds and Jim Perrin's little Jack Russell.

And another thing, the changing rooms are always so hot that the whole blinking affair is made even more miserable by the hot house effect. You sweat and strain your way out of your street clothes, and bung on whatever it is you're buying, waddle out of the changing room to stand redfaced, dripping and bedraggled in front of the mirror, and some weird stranger stares back at you looking as though he's been dressed by burglars. I don't know what it is about mirrors in clothes shops but I'm sure they're made by the same people who make fun fair mirrors. Am I alone in this? Am I the only person in the world who goes to buy a duvet jacket or a pair of salopettes who sees himself in the mirror and thinks, 'Who is that ugly little fat bugger over there?'

In fact writing this has got me so wound up about the whole business that I'm going to have another go at mending the split breeks. Sod Guy Fawkes he can go bare bum to the bonfire for all I care.

There is a festival of mountaineering writing in the early part of next year to which I'm hoping to go. Not as a mountain writer you understand, my little squibs are merely musings on the touchline from someone who wanders in the hills in the same way he wanders in his head, without too much thought or purpose. But I would like to go just to meet other writers. Writing is such a lonely occupation. There we all sit in our little rooms banging away at the micro chips, eyes bleary from the VDU, probably getting all kinds of radiation sickness or whatever from these machines we work on, a solitary vice much like that other one the holy fathers used to warn me off all those years ago. I wonder about the people one might meet at such a gathering – Chris Bonington, Doug Scott, Dermot Somers, Roly Smith and of course the legendary Arnold Crunchbucket whose description of the first ascent of Gunghapooch is a classic of mountaineering literature. Who, having read it, can forget his account of the last night the two companions spent huddled together at high camp?

We clung to each other for warmth in the snowhole as outside the blizzard raged. A terrible night. Smithers' hot water bottle burst, and I dropped the Horlicks tablets into the snow. Smithers bent over to retrieve them and his head fell off. It was the worst case of frostbite I had ever seen, poor beggar. Yet when the dawn broke and the blizzard abated things somehow took on a different light, and we set off for the summit. I with my feet in my pocket, Smithers carrying his head. I knew then what it was to be an Englishman.

April, 1996

Gin Gan Gooly – Part One

I got a bit annoyed the other day when I read an article in one of our major newspapers attacking the Boy Scout movement. Now I've no particular love for organisations of any kind, and believe with Groucho Marx that I ought to be deeply distrustful of any club that would consider having me as a member, but I've got to speak up in defence of the Boy Sprouts. I hated the flag saluting, the church parades and the God is an Englishman attitude of much of the movement, but I managed to ignore most of that, and my years as a scout took me into the hills and mountains of this island and gave me a love of the high lands that is still with me.

The industrial ghetto of Lower Crumpsall where I spent my childhood didn't have much in the way of roaring cataracts or beetling crags, though it did have roaring factory hooters and a beetling dye works. The dye works by the way was the biggest in Europe, and the river that ran through what had once been a beautiful green valley, and was now a red brick canyon, changed colour more frequently than the Tories change ministers, going from bright red to deep purple in minutes. If you fell in that river you didn't drown, you got poisoned, but came out a lovely colour. Sitting having your dinner you would look out of the window and see a yellow dog chasing a bright green cat down the road. A colourful childhood.

But the Scouts changed all that, giving me my first taste of the Great Outdoors, and material for several comedy routines. At my first camp in the wilds of Ashworth Valley, a sooty moorland dale no more than a handful of miles north of Manchester, I was put in charge of the beans. We were cooking beans and sausage for sixty, and I had two massive dixies of *thunderberries* in my care. The fire began to die, and nothing I could do would revive it, weeks of summer rain had drenched all the woods around so that most of our fuel was sodden, and our fires smoked and sulked more than your average teenage daughter. A thin drizzle fell continuously as I fed the almost moribund fire with damp sullen faggots. Lacklustre wreaths of smoke curled round the blackened bottom of the dixie. I stuck my finger in the beans, they weren't even lukewarm. My pal Pete who was in charge of the bread and butter, and was smearing something yellow on one hundred and twenty slices of something damp and white, looked up from his work under the tarpaulin.

'Best thing is to tell Skip, he'll get it going.'

I sent word to Skip that the fire was going out and he appeared striding manfully across the field with a jerry can of paraffin. 'This'll get it going,' he stated forcefully, shaking a good gallon of fuel on the fire, splashing at least two pints of it into the beans along the way. 'Now, who's got the matches?'

What happened next still makes me chuckle years later. The fire, sulky though it was, was still hot enough to turn the paraffin into a gas, and when Skip threw the match in there was a sudden *whooshing* noise, and Skip lost his eyebrows and his cow-lick and singed his woodsman's thong. All of us wanted to laugh but none of us did, we didn't fancy peeling potatoes for the next fortnight.

The fire was roaring now, sending flames twenty feet into the air and setting fire to Pete's tarpaulin. By the time we'd sorted things out the beans were bubbling, and the sausages were hissing like angry anacondas, sending delicious waves of sausage smell into the dank summer air. Fifty plus scouts appeared from nowhere banging on their tin plates. I noticed a thin skin of oil on top of the beans and decided to stir it in. Beans are bad enough at the best of times, beans with paraffin sauce proved a nouvelle cuisine too far, but the cold and hungry scouts didn't notice. (Either that or they thought that Skip had bought *off* beans on purpose as part of his Ford Popular fund-raising drive).

That night the camp looked like a glowworm's nest as close on sixty loose-bowelled scouts scurried round with torches looking for a vacant latrine, the smaller ones were weeping a little, some of them calling for their mothers. Only Pete and I who had seen the paraffin go in the beans, and had stuck to sausage sandwiches, got a good nights sleep.

There were other things that made that camp memorable: the ghost stories we told each other every night until we were all gibbering idiots ready to scream at the slightest noise; the discovery that there was something strange about Skip in that he was very keen to see us all with our clothes off and insisted on us skinny dipping every morning and evening in the river that ran by the camp. He also checked us out frequently for heat rashes – in the middle of the coldest, wettest August anybody could remember.

But what I remember best about that camp and others like it in the Lake District, and on the edge of Dartmoor is the walking and the climbing, the mountains and the moors. To a kid from the smoggy streets of Manchester it was paradise. There were moments of almost transcendent happiness: climbing gritstone crags, rambling along lakeland ridges, and swimming, at the end of the day, in still river pools where willows bent over the water and midges drove us howling along the bank, towels flapping; and there were the camp fires and the singing.

All small beer now I suppose in these days of Nintendo and Power Rangers, but there was more magic in those summer camp days than in a million Super Marios. More power to the Boy Sprouts, their knobbly knees and their gin gan goolies.

March, 1996

Gin Gan Gooly – Part Two

I spent a few days walking in the hills of Connemara this summer, revisiting the Twelve Bens and the Maumturks which are surely amongst the most glorious hills in the world. And it was while climbing steadily up to Maumeen that a damn tune got into my head, and wouldn't get out all day. I don't know if this happens to you, but once I get my walking pace set, I nearly always end up with some melody or another wobbling around inside my head. (Please tell me I'm not alone, and that I don't have to leave my brains to medical science as a world oddity). For some damn reason on this particular walk the first two lines of *On The Good Ship Lollipop* got in the dusty cupboard of my brain and rattled around there for ages like a skeleton with St. Vitus' Dance.

On the good ship Lollipop
It's a short trip to the candy shop
Where (something something something)
On the (something something) Peppermint Bay.

I tried everything: thinking lewd and erotic thoughts involving nuns, waffle irons and a bath full of custard; holding my breath; deliberately singing every catchy tune I knew including *Yellow Submarine* and *The Dicky Bird Song* but, when I wasn't looking the flaming lollipops would start up again conjuring up visions of that curly headed brat that sang it in the film lollipopping about on some boat or other.

T. S. Eliot (the only poet I know who's name is an anagram of toilets) wrote in *The Waste Land* about sensing that, though you are alone in a strange landscape, you can often sense that there is somebody walking beside you. Well in my case it's a scrum of people walking beside me and they're all singing rubbish songs. I once climbed Ben Bulben with the words, *Rent me a car Dan Dooley*, going through my head to the tune of Tom Dooley, because the rental firm I'd used had belonged to the aforementioned Dan. I once climbed Kilimanjaro keeping time to *Una Paloma Blanca* and once sat in the rain in Baltistan for four days, staring out at a slowly dissolving landscape as *Come On Baby Light My Fire* ran through the corridors of my mind like a dose of Epsom Salts through a Bactarian camel.

One of the worst times was when I was walking in the Pennines somewhere (I think it was above Mankinholes) and perhaps because of old associations (days out with the Boy Sprouts etc.) that damn Gin Gan Gooly song climbed in through the window of the head and started running around the brain like a one legged man in a bum kicking competition. All day my inner voice was singing:

Gin gan gooly gooly gooly gooly watcha,
Gin gan goo gin gan goo.
Heyla heyla sheyla
Heyla shayla heyla ho!
Shally wally, shally wally, shally wally, shally wally,
Umpa, umpa, umpa, umpa

This load of rubbish was drummed into me from the tender age of eleven at scout camp when, after having been dragged across Dartmoor, Ashworth Valley or the Langdale Pikes in the rain and mud and cold, we would be fed baked beans and skinless sausages and made to sit round a smoking campfire in the drizzle looking cheerful, smiling and whistling in the face of all difficulties, and singing the above drivel.

For years that damn song has plagued me. The tune is abysmal and only beaten in the abysm stakes by the *Dicky Bird Song* and most of Andrew Lloyd Webber, but I can't get it out of my head. I can hear it now running round gin-gan-goolying. And what do the words mean?

Well after years of research the scientific community have come up with the following – nobody knows. Learned linguists and anthropologists confess themselves foxed. Many have come to the conclusion that it is of Afrikaans origin and that Baden Powell picked it up in Bloomfontein on the same night he picked up his famous rash. Rubbish.

Well I have the answer. After yonks of head pummelling and meditation, with some help from *The Boys Own Book Of Cryptography* I have mastered the secret of the Gin Gan Gooly business.

Any of you gentle readers who live north of the Tweed will know that *Gin* is Scots dialect for 'If' while *Gan* of course means 'To Go'. A gooly is not a testicle as some have averred, but a ghost as in the old Scots poem, *From ghosties and ghoulies and things that go bump in the night.* The first lines therefore read:

> *If you go ghostie, ghostie, ghostie, ghostie,*
> *If you go, if you go.*

The ghost in question is I am certain no ghost at all, but refers to a lady with a pale skin. This is repeated and then the singer switches from Scots to Liverpudlian.

Hey la, means, 'Excuse me sir or madam.' As in *Hey la, 'av yer ad yer connie onny butty?* (Trans. Have you dined my friend?')

This is followed by an Australian word, *Shayla* which is Oz talk for a lady.

Shally wally, as any student of Bill Chaucer and Eric Shakespeare knoweth, is Old Middle English for shall we, will we? While *Umpa umpa* is a universally recognised euphemism for sexual congress.

The whole song therefore is an invocation to a pale skinned lady not to part from the singer, but instead to stay and indulge in sexual congress. What the Boy Scout movement are thinking of teaching this to children I do not know, and I take this opportunity to warn the powers that be at Baden Powell House that if this tune runs round my brain one more time I will sue them for musical abuse.

September, 2003.

Lost in Liverpool

There are times in your life when you don't need drugs, when things all around you seem so strange that a sniff of a barmaid's apron would send you into orbit, and being in the same room as an antihistamine tablet would give you visions of madonnas on gable end walls, and moving statues crying genuine tears. Maybe it's my hormones, but recently every day has been like that. I went to Ireland a few days back and felt, for most of the week, as though I was in a strange European Art Film – *Being John Malkevitch* meets *Darby O'Gill And The Little People* – sort of thing.

To begin with there was Liverpool. If Einstein had ever come in off the M62 to try and find the Dublin Ferry at the Pier Head, then he would have torn up his Theory Of Relativity and written another one called The Theory Of Elasticity, because Liverpool is an elastic city. I must have travelled on that ferry dozens of times, and yet each time the signs have sent me a different way. Once you used to be able to drive straight through the city towards the Liver Building, then turn up the dock road for the Pier Head. Then somebody with a degree in Urban Confusion decided to send us via Ormskirk and the tomato fields of Lancashire. The city Highway Authority eventually realised how stupid that was after entire families, unable to find any more signs that would lead them back to the Mersey and the Dublin boat, gave up and settled down to spend the rest of their lives in benders at the side of the radish fields.

So they made it slightly better, and only sent us out to Maghull, ten miles north. Then, just when I'd got used to that, they started sending us directly towards the Pier Head but cunningly steered us away at the last moment (like some fiendish Spanish bullfighter) round a lot of abattoirs, fat rendering, and lung, liver and lights factories. Now I know dockland approaches are never glamorous, but is it necessary to send us on our holidays hubcap deep through gore, gristle and eyeballs?

Last week it wasn't so much the way the signs sent us as the distances shown on them.

Pier Head – one and a half miles, one read. Two miles later another sign said *Pier Head – one and a half miles,* forty minutes and lots of dark gangster filmish streets later we saw the Liver Birds in the far distance, and a sign told us we were still a mile and a half from the Pier Head. Wisely I had allowed several days for the trip from the Yorkshire Dales to Liverpool, and did in fact find that I needed most of them. Whatever time-space continuum Liverpool is on it doesn't quite link up with the rest of the world.

When I got to the Pier Head and the ferry port I was overwhelmed as always by the high quality of the catering services. The only tea available came from a machine. It would have given ulcers to an industrial boiler, made my teeth ache, and my ginger moustache turn a sort of verdigris colour. The boat trip was four hours, and was spent in the company of a lot of sea anglers. Now I go fishing myself, for the pot you understand, and some of my best friends are anglers, so I'm not having a moan here. But, one sea angler I can take, three sea anglers are just about bearable, but forty or more sea anglers, all talking in loud voices and at the same time about conger and bass while getting off their heads on Guinness at half past eight in the morning is hard to bear. I found it very difficult to concentrate on my Marcel Proust I can tell you.

The drive across Ireland was as long and tedious as ever, and Einstein must have been here too because two hundred and three kilometres felt more than five hundred miles. It went on and on and on. Ireland is one of the most beautiful countries in the world yet somehow has managed to fill its midlands with GIBA – *Great Irish Bugger All.* I ploughed on through the GIBA, and arrived in Connemara in the late afternoon without any more incidents other than navigating the two hundred roundabouts around Galway, and a herd of wild goats that had all decided to have sex on the road at

Maam Cross. As I drove the last miles to the house, the sun was shining on the Twelve Bens and a glorious Paul Henry sky hung over Connemara – wonderful stuff.

The next morning, having checked that the stray cat that appeared a few weeks back hadn't got into the house and had her kittens in my Tilley hat, I packed my rucksack and set off for a short walk up the hill across the bay. It's an easy walk from the beach along a bohareen, and up a steep hill to what was once a signal tower but is now a heap of rubble on the windy summit. On the seaward foot of the hill is a holy well, and I set off down aiming for it, but obviously Einstein and the Liverpool planners had been here and they'd shifted it because I couldn't find it. I must have drunk from it a dozen times over the years but it wasn't there – it was in a state of goneness. There is a wonderful wild and lonesome Irish tune called *Paddy's Rambles In The Park*, said to have been learned by the Donegal fiddler John Docherty. He walked into a field one night, not knowing that there was a fairy fort in it, and he wandered around for hours lost, hearing fairy music coming from underground. When daylight came, and he saw his way out of the enchanted field, he had the tune fixed in his head. Well either Einstein, the Liverpool Sign Writers or the fairies had moved that holy well, because it was not there no more.

To cap it all, after a week in the hills, I headed back across GIBA to the boat, and there were the fishermen still going on about cod and ling and conger, and they got sloshed, and took out a fluffy toy leprechaun with a ginger beard the colour of ferry-port tea. They pressed a switch in its belly, and it sang *When Irish Eyes Are Smiling* for four and a half bloody hours while the boat rocked and the fishermen drank, only it felt like four and a half pigging years because the Leprechaun had Einstein's pigging voice. I'd recognise it anywhere

July, 2003.

Return Tram Ticket to Annapurna Please

My late father-in-law spent the years 1939 to 1945 doing his best to stop a small man with a toothbrush moustache from replacing our national dish of fish and chips with shweinhaxe mitt sauerkraut. My father-in-law's part in this battle against a uni-testiculate, failed watercolourist was played out in an old wooden hulled trawler that had been converted into a minesweeper. He was a radio operator who spent most of the war tapping out signals on a morse key as the skipper took them round places like the Bay of Capri, sweeping mines with (one must presume) a big but very soft brush. *What has this got to do with mountains Harding you procrastinating wordsmith?* I hear you squeal with impatience. Hold your water, all will become clear.

The skipper of the minesweeper always began each tour of duty by holding up a tram ticket. It was the return ticket from the docks back to his home. *As long as I've got this we're going to get back lads*, he used to say. And he was right; they always did get back. And, in a way, unlike some of the people I've trekked and climbed with over the years, I've always had that return tram ticket – so far, at least.

I've never done anything particularly brave or foolhardy – but, then again, you don't have to be bivvied out on a vertical wall of bad rock and ice in a massive storm to buy the farm. On one trip to the Khumbu Glacier many years back, thirty six trekkers and locals died in one of the worst post-monsoon storms ever to hit that valley. We wandered through the mess and the tragedy a few hours later, safe and sound, except for a bad case of Gandhi's Revenge which I'd contracted in Kathmandu. Another time, in Pakistan, a few days after we had made it back to Skardu following hours of hell and high boredom on the Karakoram Highway, a

Jeep carrying six trekkers was swept off the road by an avalanche and ended up, driver and passengers and all, being ground into sludge by the thundering waters of the river in the gorge far below. I could go on – and I sometimes do – about the near misses or lucky escapes that I've had, but I won't.

Because lucky escapes you can do nothing about – if your name is on the boulder or jeep – then it's kismet and kiss your bottom goodbye. (I've just found out by the way that when he was dying Lord Nelson didn't say, *Kiss me Hardy!* but, *Kismet Hardy!* i.e. *It's fate Hardy – my name was on that sharpshooter's bullet.* And for years I thought Horatio was a Friend of Dorothy. It just goes to show. However, I digress.)

What I want to say is that it isn't the big stuff, the Kismet that you can do nothing about that irks me, but the small stuff you find in the great outdoors that makes life a dreary miserable affair at times: midges, mosquitoes, leeches, bad food, piles, splinters, blisters, itchy bits, shut pubs, and moaning members. (The last by the way is not an obtuse reference to genitalia but refers to other trekkers in the group.)

I think one of my most miserable experiences was in the Khumbu valley on the walk in from Jiri. We were heading for Mera peak, five of us, assorted climbers and cavers. The weather was terrible. It was late October and the monsoon, which should have been finished weeks ago, was still in full flow –and monsoon in Nepal doesn't just mean wet, it means leeches. Now I know that symbiosis is just part of nature, and that things that batten on to other creatures and make their lives a misery: lamprey, midges, politicians, lawyers, architects, planners, etc. are just part of the Blind Watchmaker's grand design. But that doesn't mean I have to like it. And leeches, bloody leeches, bloody, pigging, sodding leeches are one of the Blind Watchmaker's worst ideas.

In the jungles of Nepal they hide under the leaves of the trees along the trail waiting for humans or animals to pass. They have some kind of receptor that senses blood warmth, and they can swing themselves off the leaves and onto your flesh in a wink. And they get everywhere, not just on exposed flesh: up the legs of your pants, down your socks, in your underwear, up your sleeves, down the neck of your shirt. Every hour or so we'd have a leech stop and pull the little buggers off. Don't believe that rubbish about them leaving their heads inside you, they don't.

There was one night when I got in my tent after dinner, the rain lashing down, the ground sodden, the tent sodden, everything sodding sodden, and began, for a bit of light entertainment, to remove my leeches. I lost count at twenty. I gathered them all in my tin mug and threw them out of the flap. Snuggling down in the sleeping bag I turned off my head torch, and got ready for a good night's leech-free kip. Then I heard the mouse. It was scrabbling around inside the tent. Bugger, bugger, bugger. I switched on my head torch. The muesli bar I'd left on my kit bag was half gone, but of the mouse there was no sign. I switched off my head torch and lay back down. Scrabble, scrabble, scrabble, went its little claws on the ground sheet. Sod it. I was tired, I was fed up, I wanted to go to sleep. Bugger the mouse. I tried to sleep, lying on my back, willing myself into unconsciousness.

Just as I was slipping deep into a dark pool of dreams the mouse ran across my face. My screams woke the camp up, and the next camp, and several villages downstream. I switched my torch on, and there it was, splayed against the tent flap – terrified, the size of my thumb. I picket it up by the tail and threw it out, hoping that the leeches would get it. Bad stuff, horrible stuff at the time. But at least I didn't die, there's no cairn with a wooden plaque on it saying 'M. Harding 1944-1983. Killed By A Mouse.' – and why? Because I had the return ticket. In fact I've still got it, somewhere. Now where did I put it?

November, 2005.

Lord Lucan's Concertina

Some of you may remember a modicum of kerfuffle, I was involved in a while back when a dead mate of mine was mistaken for Lord Lucan. It was a small literary dust up concerning a book called *Dead Lucky*, which claimed that Lucky Lucan had ended his days as a hippy living on the beach at Goa, naming him as Jungly Barry. Never was an investigation so comically wrong. The lad in question (who was known both as Jungly Barry and Mountain Barry) was not Lord Lucan but Barry Halpin. He was of Irish descent, came from St. Helens, Lancashire, and his Irishness was about the only possible link there could have been with Lord Lucan, since in every other respect Barry was the antithesis of that murdering Hooray Henry. (The Lucan estate by the way still owns most of the town of Castlebar in County Mayo and the people have refused to pay their rent ever since Lucky vanished saying they'll pay up when he comes to collect it in person).

Barry was a socialist of the old school, a republican with a small 'r', who didn't believe in violence, and a great folk musician whose knowledge of Irish traditional music was amazing. He could play concertina, banjo, tin whistle, flute, guitar, mandolin and banjo and could play them all really well; as I wrote in a poem I made about him, *He could get a tune out of a potato.* He was also a fine singer with a great fund of songs many of which he'd collected himself on field trips around Ireland, and I still have some tapes he left behind of traditional musicians he had recorded such as Willy Clancy and Packie Russell.

He trained as a teacher, and taught for a good few years in Lancashire, hitchhiking round these islands during the holidays singing in folk clubs, sleeping on floors and under hedges, and generally having a good time. One year he made his way to

Australia via India, and fell in love with India because it was a much more spiritual place than St. Helens. He decided to spend the rest of his life in Goa where it seemed to be always summer-time, the booze was cheap and the living easy. He lived a simple life, drinking and playing in bars, taking people on trips into the jungle, coming home occasionally to stay with his sister in St. Helens and to go to hospital for treatment for the liver condition which would eventually kill him. When he died his friends didn't (as the book asserts) give him a *Viking burial,* he was cremated pretty much as everybody else is in India when they die, and his ashes were scattered into the ocean.

He lived and died as he wanted: an outsider loved by many, and remembered by any whose lives he glanced against on his orbit through time. His niece and last surviving relative, who lives in North Carolina, emailed me to say she had seen the pictures in the book, and was one hundred per cent certain that they were not of the dark haired and slippery Lucky Lucan, but of her gingery haired, bearded, heavy drinking, hippy, traditional musician, uncle, Barry Halpin. I also got phone calls from musicians all over the country (including half the Liverpool Ceilidh band) all of them laughing dementedly to think that Barry had been fingered as a millionaire who killed his children's nanny.

The reason I'm telling you all this is that Barry, as well as being a fine musician, was also a climber and hillwalker who climbed (in North Wales and the Lakes in particular) to a very high standard. He was one of the crowd who would congregate in places like The Old Dungeon Gill in Langdale to sing and laugh the night away after a good day on the hill. He was one of that band of anarchic outsiders who saw the mountains as a symbol of our freedom, and who saw their sport as an affirmation of the bond between Man's soul and the planet. There were so many in those days, climbers, hill-walkers and cavers alike, who saw what they did not as a consumer exercise: wearing the right gear, ticking off the summits or the hard routes; but as something which brought them closer to the Real. We don't seem to have as many characters these days; men and women who weren't just larger than life but were Life affirming. Perhaps because we don't meet so much in the old pubs any more, perhaps because we've become more concerned with trying to make a living, with staying ahead of the credit card.

Who is there now like Geoff Woods who once got thrown out of the Old Dungeon Gill for reciting bawdy poetry only to climb back in through the minuscule toilet window and start all over again before being thrown out again. If I remember rightly the poem was *The Great Farting Contest At Shitum On Peas,* no more bawdy than Chaucer's *The Miller's Tale.*

Who is there now like Bob Spray and Fish Jim? Bob once climbed up the flagpole of Whitby Abbey, and stuck a chamber pot on the top, and Fish Jim, who wore the worst ginger wig you've ever seen, would think nothing of climbing in the Lakes all day, singing and drinking all night, then driving back to Hull in the morning to work on the fish docks. He was also an enthusiastic (if not tuneful) singer whose version of *Bogie's Bonny Belle* still rings in my ears. He was a terrible man for fighting too, and if a ruckus started was always one of the first in. The sight of his ginger wig flying out of the door of The Green Dragon at Hardraw Force in the Yorkshire Dales one night will live with me till I die.

Proust asked, *Where are the snows of yesteryear?* I ask, *Where are the Fish Jims, the Geoff Woods, the Bob Sprays and Jungly Barrys of yesteryear?* They can't all be Lord Lucan, or Jack The Ripper, or Shergar, or the crew of the *Marie Celeste* - can they?

November, 2003

Making Hay While the Chicken Knits

I'm a great fan of the animator Nick Parks, creator of *Wallace and Grommit, Creature Comforts* and *Chicken Run.* He is, I believe, a genius, and one of the few good things to come out of Preston. Those who have seen *Chicken Run* might remember that the chickens on the farm steadfastly and determinedly refused to accept that they were going to end up with a potato and carrot jump-suit and a hot pastry overcoat courtesy of the major industrial strength pie machine in the next compound. One chicken (who knitted a lot) thought any chicken that vanished had gone on its holidays.

It came to me, as I walked under Pen y Ghent yesterday, and watched four Land Rovers chew up the old bridleway that leads up from the Crown at Horton, that we are all a little like that knitting chicken.

I remember when I was a kid of seven being taken by a civil engineer who was the friend of a neighbour, to see an open-cast coal mine he was working on. It was a lovely summer's day, and I can remember, with total recall, the rap and rant of the diesel, the stink of the exhaust and the thick black fumes flying into the blue sky; and I remember looking at the torn earth of what until then had been Lancashire meadow lands, and feeling in my gut that this was all terribly, terribly wrong. Years later while trekking in Ladakh, I learned that Buddhists don't mine and quarry the earth because they believe it wounds it, and though I'm not naive, and understand that we need stone for building, lime for mortar, and oil to keep us going for the next few years at least, I also know that the seven year old boy I once was had it right. There is something very, very wrong in what we're doing to our world.

Ice islands the size of Wales break off from the Antarctic Shelf; polar bears are forced to come as far south as Rotherham because they can't find food or a shag; scorpions are now nesting just south of Milton Keynes, and there are enough growth hormones flying round the planet in the food chain to make us all seventeen foot tall and fertile at six years of age. GM crops have already discovered how to climb through barbed wire fences, no matter how pollen proof we make them, so it won't be long before cross-species fertilisation takes place, and all we need to do to make an Irish Stew is get hold of a sheep that's been crossed with a potato, an onion and a carrot. Should be simple enough, they've been making bananas that taste of strawberries for years. Ah, and yet we knit, and yet we knit.

'Windfarms', someone shouts, and, to a man, New Labour jumps up and down and waves its jockeys in the air. Yet the world knows that windfarms are not the answer, not on mountain tops anyway. The amount of energy needed to make the machine in terms of metalwork, plastics and wiring, together with the amount of energy needed to build the roads up the mountain to get it there, and the machines to build the roads, and the diesel to fuel those machines, far outweigh any savings to the planet. The only reason they are being foisted on us is because there are grants to aid developers and because the electricity companies (who are they this week?) are forced to buy this Green Power at a rate favourable to the developers. Greenpeace and Friends of the Earth should be spending more time shouting for conservation, and less for wind farms. If we all turned off lights that weren't vital in our homes, if we washed the pots by hand instead of letting them pile up for a week in the dishwasher, if we didn't have so many unneeded city lights, we'd save gigawatts of power.

When the Tories were in, the then minister for the environment said, re-windfarms, that the National Parks mustn't think that they would automatically be thought exempt from windfarm development. So there you have it. What the Tories thought yesterday Blair pretends is the new exciting third way of today. There are plenty of people who think windfarms are attractive, but they tend to be people who think wilderness is something to be tamed and exploited. Call me an elitist if you like, but I think that landscape, like music and poetry is something we need, something that can make us more real, can put us in touch with something more than Junior Big Brother, Changing Gardens or Family Swap or whatever other piece of junk the cynical no-marks who run the Haunted Fishtank dream up next.

Cameron McNeish wrote recently that he wouldn't want the kind of artificial aids we find in the Via Ferratas to make their way into our wilderness regions.

If the money grubbing charlatans that run this country now could get away with it there'd be funiculars on every hill taking us up to a windfarm, café and play area complete with souvenir shop and llama rides. Cynical moi! You bet your donkey (or ass – whichever is nearest). We spend a lot of time and energy in the outdoor movements of these islands fighting desperate battles against the Knitting Chickens that run this planet: Blair and Bush knit their way through various eco-summits while the big boys at the back – the Christian, neo-con fundamentalists who believe there can't be an ecological disaster because (and I quote) *God wouldn't allow it* – get on with raping and polluting the earth.

We live on a small, non-renewable planet. If we settled for one car that would last a lifetime, clothes that don't need to be replaced every time somebody decides flares are back in/out, washing pots by hand and not eating anything bigger than our heads then we might have hills that our children can walk on and beaches our grandchildren can play on. But not if the grinning fools that run the planet at the moment get their way. When I argue with the Panglossians who think we can go on for ever taking from the Earth, they tell me to get real. I studied enough history at Uni to know what Realpolitik means. It means letting the piemakers get their way while the chicken knits.

December, 2003

Proust and the Skirting Board

I bought a pedometer a while back because I was curious as to how far I walked in a normal day, not just on the hills but doing things like going to the shops, mooching around, walking about the house, etc. When I worked it out I was quite amazed; a couple of trips to the pub and the shops had clocked up six miles, and they're only round the corner. Mind you I did get lost both times coming back from the pub – I've only been going there for twenty years. Walking around the house was interesting too, since I now get into pretty much every room I go to having forgotten why I set off there in the first place. I usually walk off to get something: a stapler, a CD, an egg whisk, pair of socks or such, see something en route that distracts me: the scratches on the sofa the cat has done, that piece of loose skirting I always mean to nail back into place but never do, the wine glasses I left out last night and meant to wash and put away; then I arrive in the room I set out for and I've forgotten what I set out to do in the first place.

Chairman Mao (stealing the words from a far greater Chinese philosopher, Chou Mai Fat) once said, *A journey of a thousand miles starts with a single step.* Very true – and you could add to that, *It will either rain or go dark by nightfall.*

In any case these old saws and sayings are all very fine, but I bet that Mao never forgot what he was supposed to be doing when he began The Long March. He didn't get to Peking having been distracted by a loose piece of skirting board or the cat washing it's nether regions on the window sill. He didn't arrive in the Forbidden City and shout, *Can anybody remember what the xing hell we're doing here? I was busy watching that cat wash its whatsits.*

And what about Alexander the Great? I bet he didn't get to the banks of the Indus and turn round to his Hellenic blond mates and say, *Giz a clue? I've forgot what we've come for. Disembowelling all them Tartars and nailin' that skirtin' board back 'as put it right out of me 'ead.* And by the way, unless you are a military historian in thrall to human juggernauts who crush everything in their path, there was nothing Great about Our Alex. He was a murderous, rapacious, drunken thug who had a permanent harem of 365 women (what did he do in a leap year?) and yet still preferred small boys. He butchered thousands upon thousands of innocents, whole cities, to the last woman and child; and numberless fine buildings, temples and palaces were torched by him and his gangs of killers. In any case he inherited his great cavalry from his father, and left behind very little but for some curiosities: a number of very blond people called the Kafir Kailash in the Hindu Kush (the Macedonians were blond) and a lot of strangely pleasing stone Buddhas on the banks of the Oxus that are robed like Greek statues.

It wasn't that young Alex was a Buddhist: some of the Greek stone masons he dragged along to carve commemorative statues of himself wherever he went on his plunderings and murderings went AWOL and settled down with the local girls. No – but me no ifs – he was an out and out monster. Alexander the Great? I suppose, if Hitler had had his way, and hadn't stopped to fix that skirting board, historians of the future would be talking about Adolph the Great, and the good burghers of Ecclefechan would be eating bratwurst and wearing leather shorts to this very day.

And talking of leather shorts; how is it that you can't get proper shorts nowadays, only a pair of things that look like cut down clown's trousers? Not only are we using up all that cotton unnecessarily: the baggier the shorts the higher the wind drag, as any schoolboy or girl could tell you. When I go for a walk on a sunny day I want to expose all my legs to the old currant bun, not just the four inches of flesh between the bottom of the shorts and sock top. Yet I go in my local outdoor store and all I can find are huge baggy things that make me look like that little fat bloke, you know the one

I mean, Lofty, the Welsh one who couldn't sing in *It Ain't Half Hot Mum* – I think that's what the programme was called. What was I talking about? Shorts, that was it. Perhaps I ought to found the Campaign For Real Shorts.

And talking about real things. What's happened to our winters? *Where are the snows of yesterday?* Proust once wrote, and he should know. He got so worried about it he used to keep snowballs in his fridge behind the dried up cheese and the gone-solid jar of Privet Blossom Honey. And he's right, when I was a nipper it started snowing in December, you got chilblains and chapped legs, made slides in the playgrounds, made snowmen in the yard, and sledged in the park; the snow lasted for ages, and there was lots of it, white stuff and very cold. Last winter round our way there was an afternoon of some grey stuff that the cats looked at with wonderment, then it all went away.

Well, like baggy shorts, this is something up with which we should not be putting! And what about Global Warming? What are we doing about it? About as much as we're doing about baggy shorts.

What we need to do is stop driving now – all of us – this minute. Get out of your car and throw away the key. Now. Then, not only would George Bush and Dick Cheney and the Saudi Royal family and the Bin Ladens go bankrupt, we would all have to walk everywhere and we'd be a lot healthier and we could all wear pedometers to see how far we'd walked.

Pedometers? That's strange. I started this piece off talking about pedometers but I've forgotten where it was supposed to be leading. It must have been that loose skirting board.

October, 2004

Three Bits of String and a Knuckle

I bought a pedometer thingy recently and it has come in extremely handy for settling arguments. I'm the bloke in our loose group of walkers who sorts the routes out, gets everybody up by standing at the bottom of the stairs whistling and screaming, and generally acts as Ubergrupenwalkerfuhrer. The only thing I don't do is force them to sing the Horst Wessel song as we ramble along the mountain tracks. I'm not a born leader. I'm not a born follower either. I suppose (if a counsellor were to get a grip of me) I would be described as something of a solitary. But faced with a house full of people who've all said they want to go for a walk tomorrow and who, when tomorrow comes, also want to lie in bed for an extra hour – what do you do? Well you do what I do and stand at the bottom of the stairs in your socks shouting and moaning until they get up, eat their breakfast, and get their boots on.

The rows always come later, and are always to do with the distance covered. *That must have been eighteen miles!* one of them moans as he takes off his steaming socks to show a cluster of blisters the size and colour of snooker balls. *That was never twelve miles!* another one grumbles, laying a shoelace along the route on the map then measuring it against the scale at the bottom.

In the old days we used to take out the map-measurer to settle the quarrel but the problem is that map measurers are universally rubbish; the little wheels slip and the scale that you read off is all different colours for different scale maps so that in the end, having walked twelve miles, it comes up as either two miles or three hundred and six.

Prior to the pedometer I'd relied on the *Harding Patent Span Map Measuring Method* which meant holding my index and pinky fingers in the manner of the Mediterranean cuckold insult, and then walking them along the route. Highly unscientific and highly wrong. Most of what I claimed were twelve mile easy walks were in fact twenty three mile assault courses.

So now I have the pedometer, all arguments cease. I can even tell them that the walk from home to the local Chittagong Curry House is exactly one point three miles, and none can gainsay me! The trouble is that, as with all toys for the boys, it has become a bit of an obsession.

One thing I haven't got yet is one of those satellite navigation thingies. What worries me is that the Americans are supposed to have written an error into the system so that you can only plot your position to within three hundred yards. This is to stop terrorists pinpointing American installations such as McDonald's, Stoke-on-Trent, and the Starbucks at Ecclefechan. The same technology the Americans can use to drop a cruise missile down a Baghdad kebab house air vent can take you on your merry but inaccurate way over Ilkley Moor. Three hundred yards! I would have thought that anybody with reasonable map and compass skills could get it better than that. Also, in the fog on Mweelrea Mountain in Connemara several years back, an inaccuracy of even thirty yards would have meant me walking off some very sharp bits onto a blanket of nothingness with more sharp bits at the bottom.

The other thing that concerns me is batteries. What happens if you are half way up the Boltoro Glacier and the batteries fail? At least with a compass you can always tell which way is up. And it's no use having a battery charger with you because the plug sockets on the Boltoro Glacier are all the old style: three pin, round ping, plus the voltage is dodgy. Plus another thing: what happens when all these satellites pack it in, go defunct, burn out over Piddletranthide, or land in the duck pond in Albert Park Dudley? Where will you be then? In fact that's a very good question: where will you be then? You need three or four satellites to get a good fix, and they've all got to be above the horizon at the same time. So what happens if a couple of them go out?

'Where are we oh glorious leader?'

'Well a minute ago we were in the Dolomites, but now it looks as though we are in the Golden Dragon Chip Shop in Mexborough. No we're not, we're in a massage parlour in Leith. No, we're back in Italy. Can any of you see a bloke in a skull cap waving from a balcony? It says here we're in Rome.'

I think somehow I will stick to my folded landscape and my magnetised needle. Call me an Old Luddite if you must, but I'll keep to the old ways. In any case those GPS things are damn heavy! And I've got enough to carry, apart from all the necessary things like tent and stove and clothes and sleeping bag: there's my Swiss Army Knife, my Leatherman Tool, my folding Ortlieb wash-basin, my Sony World Radio, my books for reading in the tent at night, my dictaphone, my journals, the gas powered hairdryer and styling wand (don't ask – they're not mine) and the little electric thing that gets the hairs out of your ears and nostrils.

And what happens when it's time for me to go and stand at the bottom of the stairs and get them all up? Until one of those GPS thingies learns how to do it, it's down to me to stand there shouting, *Come on! The muesli's setting like concrete and the cat's at the Linda McCartney sausages. Get your socks on and get down here – NOW – YOU 'ORRIBLE MISH MASH OF 'UMANITY!!*

When a GPS thingy has learned to do that I'll know I'm finally dispensable.

April, 2004.

First Chickens on Everest

As the Mad Granny of Grantham, Thatch the Snatch might have said, we are now a grandfather; in fact we've been a grandfather for exactly twelve months now, but since Tobias Louis lives in Virginia in the USA, we don't see nearly enough of each other. He is of course delightful with huge brown eyes, a mass of curls, six big teeth and a great smile. *Okay, enough of the soppiness already! What has this got to do with The Great Outdoors?* I hear you ask. Well this.

The other morning I was in his house in the USA as he threw his breakfast all round the room, and generally exerted his right as an individual not to eat mashed up chucky-egg and butter. So, in a desperate but doomed diversionary ploy, with my elbows wagging like a chicken's wings, and my bottom sticking out like a farthingale I sang him the chucky-egg song. You know the one, it goes:

Chick chick chick chicken lay a little egg for me,
Chick chick chick chick chicken,
Lay one for my tea;
I've not had one since Easter and now it's half past three, so
Chick chick chick chicken, lay a little egg for me.

Okay so it's hardly Lloyd Webber or Lennon – McCartney but it kept Tobias Louis amused.

It struck me, as I strutted and flapped round the kitchen dodging the flying toast and egg, that the last time I had sung this particular lieder was in Nepal while on the way back from a failed but pretty valiant attempt on Mera Peak (blizzards, crevasses and one very sick member drove us off a few hundred feet from the summit).

On our way down to Namche, our sirdar, Phu Tsering, invited us to his house for an evening of chang and music. Chang is a local rice beer and you mock it at your peril. It tastes like very watery, sour, white wine, but it has a kick like half a dozen Rooneys and three camels combined. We gathered in the house at Thyangboche just as the sun went down, shining through the small window on the burnished pots and pans that were hanging on the wall and, as the scent of burning juniper twigs drifted round the room, we drank chang and listened to Phu Tsering's wife and sister-in-law singing a slow, sad ballad about leaving a loved one behind to travel over the mountains. Other songs followed, mournful ballads about lost love, and some jolly songs from a couple of extremely good natured yak-herders in leather cowboy hats, about yak-herders chasing pretty girls. Then there was the dancing: slow dances with the men and women in line chanting and moving, as I'd seen them do years before on my first trip to the Khumbu on one never to be forgotten night, when the full moon rose over the horns of Ama Dablam, and a line of a fifty or so sherpas and sherpani danced slowly in the courtyard of the monastery at Thyangboche. Round the kitchen they went this night, winding back the years, stamping softly on the bare wooden boards of the room, small children watching from the shadows their eyes shining in the firelight. Then, when it was our turn, we sang the chicken song. With actions.

Now as somebody who presents the BBC Radio 2 folk and roots show every Wednesday 8 to 9 pm (you didn't know!) I should be hanging my head in shame at this moment (only if I did I wouldn't be able to see the keyboard of the iBook). What was I doing singing the chicken song? Even worse, what was I doing leading a group of grown men round a Sherpa kitchen at 14,000 feet above sea level, our arms flapping, our bums sticking out doing chicken impressions, singing inane drivel that doesn't even make chronological sense: Easter? Half-past three? I could always plead the chang or the altitude, but it won't do. The fact is that we didn't know any of our own national songs or dances (rugby songs and gin gan gooly do not count). The people we were with had hundreds of songs and dances to enrich their lives, we had *Chick chick chicken* and the *Okey Cokey.*

Fair enough I could have sung them some of the folk songs I know, but they're mostly about cotton mills and war, and when it comes to dancing? What we needed was a Morris team or a Lancashire clog dancer or three; what we needed was June Tabor or Kate Rusby, Maddy Prior or Nic Jones. What we had instead was five drunk blokes with beards and sunburned noses following each other round the kitchen doing the dance of the constipated chicken. Just sitting here thinking about it I am ashamed, even now, many years on.

They laughed of course. One thing I've discovered wherever I've been in the remote places on this planet: Africa, Pakistan, the Persian Gulf, Zanskar, Ladakh, is that the chicken song makes them laugh. Everybody knows what a chicken looks like, and there aren't many things funnier than watching a group of rich Westerners (who've paid in excess of two thousand pounds to come to your country to get cold and fall off mountains) staggering round clucking and warbling out of tune like very old and very sad birds whose egg-laying days are well and truly over.

The British Council will no doubt claim that they send folk singers from these islands around the world; that Morris teams from Droitwich have been seen on the streets of Ulan Bator; but that isn't the point.

Sure I can sing *Black Velvet Band, Kilgarry Mountain* and *The Wild Rover,* but they're Irish songs, and though I may sing them with some claim to authenticity because my mother's lot came from Ireland, they're not the songs people associate with England.

In fact that's a damn good question: what songs can we all sing? *Old Macdonald? Jerusalem? The Wheels on the Bus? God Save The Queen?*

Who took our songs? Was it really the aliens?

May, 2004

Far Horizons

I've been thinking long and hard about this for some time now: why do we do what we do? Why do we go out walking in the hills, scrambling up gullies in the drizzle, fighting hopeless battles with midges in the bogs of the west, pounding up snow-covered mountains in the depths of the dark days of winter? It can't be for the fame, the money or sex. I don't think I've found any of those on top of Ingleborough. I think it's something infinitely more subtle and yet infinitely simple.

I remember meeting a farmer on Achill Island a few years back, on Croghaun, one of the West of Ireland's loveliest mountains, (they want to cover it with a wind farm now, by the way). He was overtaking me, climbing steadily in an old pair of wellies with a pack of butties stuffed into his jacket pocket. I had all the best Gore-Tex gear on, a good pair of KSB and a rucksack full of goodies. After the usual stuff about lovely days and great views I said, *I bet you've been up this mountain a good few times.* His answer was short but very much on the button, *Too many f***in' times.* Point taken: he had to do it for a living, and so the joy had diminished.

Yet I bet there were times, when he stood on the top of that hill, leaving his dogs to drive the sheep down the fell, and looked around him at the Atlantic waves to his west, and the Twelve Bens of Connemara to the south, when he must surely have thought, *What a wonderful place this world of ours is and how lucky we are to be living in it.*

That's why I go walking in the hills and mountains: to be abashed by the glory of it all; to stand agog in the remote places as the trail goes on before me, leading me to peak after peak; to be humbled by the perfection of a single flower; to lie in heather listening to the music of a skylark on a moorland summer day. I don't believe in God (I had that idea beaten out of me in St. Bede's College, Manchester) but I can still stand in this world and feel whatever passes for a soul in me ringing with joy at the overpowering beauty of it all. I don't feel this way standing on the city pavements in sad November as diesel fumes choke the city, and the neon lights of McDonald's and Starbucks shine up at me out of the puddles. But I do feel this way when I'm walking a Dales river bank in October, and the land is covered with the copper and brass of fallen leaves; I do feel this way when I'm on a col in the Himalayas somewhere, looking back the way I came and looking down at the way I am to go, as the wind whips the prayer flags on the chortens on the col.

And what troubles me is that some other people don't seem to see that. They look at a landscape and think only how much money they can make out of it. A small boy once said, *an architect is a man who doesn't like fields.* There was a time when I thought this was simplistic. I'm not so sure now, sometimes the simplest things can be the truest. We live on a small island on a small planet in a remote corner of the Cosmos, yet we act as though there is no end to the land we can trash, no end to the stuff we can burn up. I look at politicians on the box and wonder if any of them realise that their words are empty air? They chunner and witter on, scoring points against each other, playing the Great Game, while outside our world is going, fading, heading for the pit. Dewey once said that, *Politics is the heavy hand big business lays upon the people.* I think it's more serious than that: Politics is like arguing about the colour of the lifeboats on the Titanic.

I read a book recently written by a Vietnam veteran who is now a Zen Buddhist monk. He murdered many people in Vietnam, most of them civilians, and he came back to America a junkie and a drunk, ending up living rough on the streets. He found peace again through meditation and through walking thousands of miles in a never ending pilgrimage, not to atone for the past, because the past is done and gone, but to understand and to bear witness to the glory of this world. And I suppose in a way this is all any of us can do: walk the hills agog at the majesty of it all and hope that one day the politicians will stop chunnering and wittering and get their boots on.

I wrote this poem after crossing the Sengi La, The Lion Head Pass, in Ladakh many years back, perhaps it explains what I feel a little better than the previous gibber.

Far Horizons

I have walked to far horizons, to
Lion-headed mountains, through
Empty lands where blood-fired
Desert ranges are still more than five
Days march away. I have watched
A mote in the far distance come my way
And turn into a running monk. I have seen
The moon slide over ice fangs
And dancers pound the earth
Under the arms of Ama Dablam.
I have left the city streets to follow that pulse
In the air that calls me still:
From Brandon to Namche, Kinder to the Hindu Kush.
I have followed the call of that ragged
Line where earth meets space,
The possible sunk deep in the core,
And to find it you let go,
Following the dream that dreams itself.

December, 2004.

Happy Harris and Geronimo's Head

I was out in the Pennines a few days back, following an old pack-horse track on the edge of Saddleworth Moor. It was the kind of summer's day you dream of, with a clear sky and hardly a breath of air stirring and, from the raw edge of the moor I could see beneath me the old mills, dye works and spinning sheds clustered in the valley: the carcass of King Cotton, the king long gone now, the mill dams that served Him strung out, like paternoster lakes, along the valley. I'm an old codger now and as an old codger I am allowed to reminisce. I draw the line however at saying, 'When I was your age' or, 'The trouble with young people today is...' because when I was their age I too thought old codgers were boring old farts, and because any trouble there might be with young people today has largely been brought about by older generations. It wasn't St Dominic's Infant School that invented the cluster bomb was it? Which teenager worried about his O-levels napalmed the villagers in Vietnam? Which seven year old girl was it that bombed Baghdad? I forget.

No I'm not that sort of old codger: I'm the sort that says, 'The first time I came here was with...' or, 'This used to be all green fields once over.'

So on that day on Saddleworth Moor my mind went back to the first time I ever walked those wild acres. I was fifteen years old, incarcerated in the local Catholic Boys Grammar School during the week, and playing lead guitar in a rock and roll band in The Dover Castle Pub at the weekends: from Friday afternoon schoolboy to a Saturday night Hank Marvin; from school milk to pints of Boddington's Bitter; is it any wonder I turned out as I did?

The drummer in the band was a lad called Les 'Happy' Harris, a tight groovemeister rock and roll drummer who worked as an optical mechanic when he wasn't sat hitting dead pigs and staring at the backsides of three pimply youths who were out front singing *Blue Suede Shoes* while grinning inanely through their acne at the pony-tailed talent. It was Happy who took me to Saddleworth.

That rock and roll summer we took a heavy ex-army tent, a few clothes, a bit of money and our boots, and got the train from Manchester to Greenfield. We took it in turns to carry the tent: a great beast of a thing with a life and a mind of its own. This tent bore grudges and settled them by getting heavier and heavier, sliding out of your arms like a lifeless drunk and coming unpacked and legging you up in no particular order. But we made it at last, away from the smoky little streets and up onto the hill, to the war memorial at Pots and Pans and set up camp, below the summit on the brow of the hill, looking out across the Chew Valley and down on the stone houses of Uppermill. According to Happy one of the rock formations across the valley was called Indian Head because, viewed from this angle it looked like – well, a Red Indian's profile. I tried my damnedest to see the noble features of a Native American in that gritstone outcrop over the way, but failed, if that was an Indian, then he'd been in a hell of a tram smash.

Oh what days they were, summertime and the living, fire and water were easy. There was a clear brook close by, bank full of the soft clean water that had made these valleys perfect for washing and dying cotton in the days of the King, and there were windfalls of wood in the copses below us. We lit the fire that night and dined on Walls Skinless Sausages, Heinz Baked Beans and mugs of strong tea; we envied no-one.

The days that followed were long, hot and glorious, and we spent them scrambling on the gritstone outcrops of the valley; roaming the moors and the ghylls and lying in the sun doing not much. I have a photograph somewhere of me, bare-chested, washing out the dixie at the stream. We were golden lads then with no knowledge of the dust that chimney sweepers and such as we must come to – and why not? As a better poet than me once wrote,

...and that is how it is:
The young are filled with light,
Why should we lay the shadows on them?

In spite of our youth we were men of the world. Happy smoked Navy Cut, and I sported a long curly pipe which earned me the nickname 'Sherlock' and which I would smoke until I got dizzy and sick. What an eedjit I was. After our skinless sausages and beans we would watch the sun go down, and sit around the camp-fire smoking like real explorers, chin wagging and rabbiting on. Then one night the talk came round to the supernatural and we put the fear of God up each other with stories of devils and vampires, boggarts and zombies. We swaggered to bed braving it out, but secretly bricking ourselves.

Later in the night we were both woken by noises outside. Something was moving round in the dark. We peeped through the laces of the door. Beyond the dying embers of our camp fire there were eyes staring at us: green eyes shining far too bright, and there seemed to be about six of them. So there we were, two rock and roll heroes, smokers and men of the world, one optical mechanic, one O-level aspirant, terrified and afraid to go out into the night to see what it was that belonged to the eyes. It wasn't sheep and there were no cows anywhere close by. In the morning the fire and our pots and pans were scattered all over the place. Happy was sure that whatever did it was malevolent. Somehow we managed to sleep the following nights and whatever it was didn't come back again.

Years later, when I wrote a book on walking in *The Peak and Pennines* I read that Pots and Pans was an old Pagan sacrificial site, and was still a site of importance to modern Pagans. When I climbed on the rock outcrops that give the place its name I found pieces of bread and flowers scattered in the pools on top of the rocks. Somebody obviously thought the place was still important.

Well, whatever it was, two of Manchester's finest rock and roll giants were like small boys wanting their mummies that night. All those years later I walked the same edge to our campsite, and stood looking out over the valley and I still hadn't a clue what it was that came to our campsite that night – and I still can't see Geronimo's Head across the valley.

The Mister Boring of the Adventurers' Club

When it comes to life-threatening experiences while trekking the Great Outdoors I must admit to being a bit of a big girl's blouse. I could make stuff up and pretend that it was only my SAS training that enabled me to survive the crossing of the Darien Swamps, but I would be lying. Apart from an avalanche on Mera Peak, and incidents with snakes in Nepal and Tanzania most of my epics have been small stuff: a lot of cows that chased me and the dog in Wensleydale; a daft landowner at the top of Wharfedale who wouldn't let me follow the footpath through his farmyard; the Kaki Skala scramble on Mount Olympus where myself and Daniel Grilloupolis felt very scared; having the runs for three weeks on the Annapurna Trek; coming across a bear in the Appalachians; the psychopath who wanted to punch my lights out in Hexham – you get the picture I'm sure: I am the Mister Boring of The Adventurers' Club.

But there's lots of niggly stuff I've had that great explorers don't get. I mean people like Captain Oates leave their tent for a short walk, turn off the GPS and vanish; people like Shipman and Tilman wander all over the Hindu Kush, fight off warlords with umbrellas and live for three months on two bowls of rice and some dried goat pizzles, and I get the little stuff.

I'm talking about the annoying stuff that sticks like an eyelash under your eyelid: too much tuna pasta on one trip in Baltistan; lumpy porridge in Lochearnhead, and very bad cramp coming off Purple Mountain in Kerry (and that was because I had been too familiar with Monsignor Guinness the night before.)

No, I have little to boast about; no scars to show and little to thrill my grandchildren with (though I can sing *The Worm At The Bottom Of The Garden* quite well). But when it comes to bad billets? Now there's a thing. When it comes to the worst B&B experiences in the world, I'm your man, and Ranulph Fiennes' experiences at the Bella Vista, Cleethorpes, pale into nothingness beside my tales of misery and despair.

There's the landlady on the South Coast Path who showed me her fresh varicose vein scars while I tried to eat my breakfast kipper with a hangover that went off the Richter Scale; there's the well-corseted, floral garbed matron who ran the Abu Graibh Guesthouse in Bakewell where there were pictures of Margaret Thatcher, Churchill and the Queen on every available wall space, and who shook her purple rinsed head at me every morning when I read the *Guardian* at the breakfast table and asked for brown toast. There was the motel in Australia where the breakfast came through a flap in the wall and consisted of some Ryvita caterers' portions of marmalade, butter, instant coffee and whitener.

After three days of the flap opening I started clucking and cheeping, and doing my best battery hen impression. The next morning the flap opened, I clucked, the tray came in. I clucked like a Rhode Island Red parting with an egg the size of a rugby ball. There was a pause, then a hairy arm followed the tray into the room and gave me the two fingered salute. And I thought Ozzies had a sense of humour!

So, when it comes to the pits, I could write the book, and may do one day. But none of them, dear reader, were as bad as the last small hotel I stayed in while walking in the mountains of Greece a couple of months back. The mice were the size of Jack Russell terriers and the bed bugs were checking out the register to see which bedroom you checked into. I'm sure it was only the woodworm holding hands that kept the building together, and the swarthy brigand who ran this menagerie would have stolen the saddle off a nightmare.

People steal my towels, he moaned. Then I discovered that the towels in the fungus-furred room where I fought a losing war with the water system for three thimblefuls of rusty sludge every morning, were all marked *The Royal General Hospital, Sydney,* souvenirs no doubt of my landlord's sojourn in that fair city.

Now before the Greek Tourist Board start writing to me, let me say that this place was a very rare exception – most of the places I stayed in Greece were excellent – but being the exception, the Costa Packet Hotel made sure it was going to be unforgettable. My bed had three legs and a pile of bricks where the other should have been, sheets the colour of a Glasgow sky in November, and probably contained enough primitive life forms to start the evolutionary process off on its own should the need ever arise.

It was one of these life forms that was the final straw that forced me to check out and go to the local health centre. Something in that rickety bed bit me. Bed bugs? Fleas? Spiders? I don't know what it was but I woke up one morning with lumps the size of golf balls all over my fair and tender body. And they itched! God how they itched! Do you remember how bad hives were when you were a kid? They were like that, only a bazillion times worse. All of this would not have been too bad if the bites were only on my ankles and back, but there were three vicious bites on my important bits, and very swollen and upset they were too. Until the day I die I will never forget standing with my trolleys round my ankles, and a Greek phrase book in my hand while a Greek doctor listened to me mangling his language.

The Greek for flea is *o psilos*, the Greek for boyfriend is *o philos*, now my Greek pronunciation isn't great and it's very easy to get words mixed up, particularly when you are in pain. Anyway I told him with a straight face that my boyfriend had bitten me on the whatsit and how he kept a straight face I will never know. At least it gave him something to tell the lads in the Taverna when he got home that night.

November, 2004.

Daddy Fox went out with a Kalashnikov

Now then, I'm no great shakes at logic (though I did have a pint once with Emmanuel Kant, and twice beat Wittgenstein at bar billiards) but let me put this to you: what's the difference between a gang of lads pouring petrol over a cat then setting fire to it, and a load of people in red jackets watching dogs tear a fox apart?

Well, since the aim in each case is to kill the animal while having fun in the process, there doesn't seem, to me, Kant or Wittgenstein to be any difference at all, QED. So I don't understand all this fuss about a ban on hunting with dogs, particularly the claim that it is an attack on the Country Way Of Life. If that were true than why didn't the CWOL come to an end when they stopped bear baiting and cock fighting? I suppose the guy who oiled the hinges of the cockpit had to go and find another job, and the bloke who towed the dead bear round the corner to the chippy, where it would be turned into Bruinburgers, had to find something else to do with his Suffolk Punch and chains, but the world didn't really come to an end, did it?

And I don't understand how anybody can call it a sport. A sport usually pits two teams against each other or individuals against each other; in each case they are usually evenly matched. Until we give the fox a kalashnikov and teach him how to shoot it, I don't see how anybody can call it a sport. And isn't there something deeply unsettling in the sight of foam-lipped, glassy-eyed, hunt supporters maintaining that banning hunting means the end of everything for the countryside and the people who live in it. Why so? The rest of us aren't allowed to pour petrol on cats and set them on fire; why should the Hon. Pru Bottysmack be treated any different? And don't trot out the old tired cliche that this is all to do with class. I wouldn't care if it was a wagon load of Kurdistan refugee, chicken-sexers chasing the fox; an act of barbarity is an act of barbarity, is an act of barbarity, as Gertrude Stein once said three times.

If a load of people of whatever class want to put red jackets on and go wobbling round the countryside with their dogs then let them; it keeps them out of mischief. But if they chase and tear apart a fox then let them be subject to the same law that punishes people who set fire to cats. And please don't tell me that the Town doesn't understand the Country. The Town understands the Country all too well. The Town understands that the Country has largely had its hand out for the last fifty years, and in terms of grants, subsidies and set-aside has had a better run for its money than the fox has ever had. The Town also understands that when It was the miners being stuffed royal by the Blessed Margaret, the Country laughed ever so quietly up its sleeve. The Town also understands that the Country shed very few tears as the fishing industry went down the pan, and the steel industry followed it only to land on top of the textile industry. The Town also understands that the Country has very largely spent the last fifty years trying to block footpaths, close down the mountains and stymie every kind of access reform that has dared to put its boots on and try and walk us into a sensible future. It is a truth worth repeating that the citizen is freer to roam at will in Russia than in this green and pleasant land, and none of us seriously doubts that the very people who scream *'Freedom'* when they want to rip up foxes will do their damnedest to block the access bill every centimetre of the way.

The other thing that waxes my wroth about the Men In Pink is the way that they jump from a ban on killing animals for fun to rural poverty and bus services, as though all three are in some way interlinked, as though an end to ripping foxes up means that all the country buses are going to de-materialise, and people who have no jobs in the countryside will have less than no jobs!

Go back ten years to when there was no threat to fox-hunting and ask where the pro-hunt lobby was then? Were they picketing the council offices demanding more buses for the little old ladies who can't get to the out of town supermarket? Did they go and kneel outside the Houses of Parliament, douse themselves with petrol and set fire to themselves in protest at the government not allowing tenants to have an automatic right to buy their tied cottages from the estate, the same right that council tenants enjoy? One thinketh not.

I've lived in the Country for more than thirty years and think that, in that time, I've come to understand it a little. The hill farmers I live amongst scrape a living from marginal land hardly managing to survive, and most of them don't care one way or another about fox hunting. If a fox is a problem on their land then they mostly take a gun and shoot it. They're more concerned about their survival on poor mountain land and their children's future in an industry that seems to be in freefall than they are about the rights of a few people to torture and kill animals for fun.

If the pro-hunt neddies are truly concerned about the Country then they can always donate a couple of days a week free labour to the hill farmers.

December, 2002.

Saluting the Flag of Lumbago

Those of you who believe, like Pangloss, that, *All is for the best in this the best of all possible worlds,* should eschew this piece, (or even esmunch it if you like) and turn over to Jim Perrin, who this month is telling you how he used to make his own bivvy bags from yogurt cartons and surgical trusses (or is it trussi?) Because this week I am about to tell you the tragic and pitiful story of how I was drummed ignominiously out of the Scouts.

You may remember that a while back I told you how I deserted from the Cub pack after a sojourn in Chorley (Africa) when our Akala got us lost in the swamps, and then expected thirty of us to live on a piece of meat the size of a dog's nose?

Well I was not long out of uniform. There was something about being a paramilitary: the camaraderie, the songs, the laughter; old ladies strewing flowers at our feet as we marched through the streets. I missed it so much that, when I was eleven, I joined the Boy Scouts, and worked my way up from Tenderfoot to Patrol Leader of the Duck Patrol in the scout troop of St. Dunstan The Aggressive, Crumpsall, Manchester.

I was very good at knots and stamp collecting, and soon collected badges in those disciplines. It wasn't long before I had my cook's, aeromodeller's, first aider's, beekeeper's, (I had three in a matchbox) and chicken-wrestler's badges. By the time I was thirteen I had that many badges that the sleeves on my uniform were trailing on the ground, and I had to wear built up shoes to keep them out of the puddles.

By the time I was fourteen, I was everything that a scout should be: clean, decent, upstanding, loyal, non-smoking, non-drinking, never gambled, led old ladies across the road, (even when they didn't want to go) and could take stones out of horses' hooves while they were galloping. Then I discovered girls on the Road To Damascus.

Well, it wasn't really Damascus, it was at The Catholic Scout Jamboree at Aylesford Priory, near Maidstone, Kent. We were there for a fortnight, full of badges, cocoa, spots and undirected testosterone. My mother was delighted that I'd gone, convinced that, being a Catholic Jamboree, there would be no chance whatever of what the priest called, *occasions of sin.* Little did my poor mother know, as she prayed for my safety, the rosary beads racing through her fingers like the anchor chain of a docking liner, that Jamborees include Girl Guides as well as Boy Scouts. We found out on the first day.

I don't know whether Time has laid a rosy veneer over those halcyon years, but not only did the sun always seem to shine in the summer holidays, not only did sherbet and mint humbugs taste much stronger, not only did anybody over thirty look incredibly old – all Girl Guides (with one exception) were fabulous looking and had big bosoms. Well there were hundreds of Girl Guides at that Jamboree, all of them (with one exception) fabulous looking with big bosoms. Many of them came from the south of England, and seemed to be entranced by our rough northern accents. At least they kept asking us to repeat things, so I can only assume they enjoyed the timbre of our argot.

We of course played up our suave northerness to the hilt and had them eating out of our hands with tales of bathtub argosies in the canal, and life threatening episodes of kick can and knock and run, eclipsing the southern Scouts completely.

One group of Girl Guides who were all (with one exception) big bosomed and fabulous looking, took an especial shine to the lads of St. Dunstan The Aggressive, and seemed to attach themselves to us. I remember one night we had a campfire sing song. There were several hundred assorted scouts and guides there, and even eagle eyed Fr. Malone, our skipper, couldn't keep an eye on us all at once. The fire flickered, casting shadows on the giant oaks of the Priory woods. The Girl Guides smiled at us winsomely, we smirked back in thrall. In the safety of the shadows the Duck patrol made its way around the fire towards the Girl Guides, all of whom were good looking with big bosoms (with one exception) That night I added the One Exception badge to my collection.

So day followed day, and night followed night, until the time came to say aloha and farewell to what was then the Garden of England, and is now twenty million acres of concrete and executive housing. The girl guides waved us farewell (with one exception) and we steamed northwards. Luckily we had a train with us.

Now I must explain that amongst our baggage was a flag that had been blessed by the Pope. I don't know whether this meant that it flapped any better or that its colours would never fade, but it had been blessed by him. I was in charge of this flag. I must also explain that when we broke camp we were all offered the contents of the grub tent. Since my family were not over-burdened with the mazoola, I took a huge tin of cocoa and two pounds of margarine for my mum. I had no room in my kitbag so I put them in the flag case. While waiting for the train my mind ran through the events of the previous two weeks, especially the bits about the bosoms. I became so distracted I forgot the flag and left it on Chatham Station. It was there for a whole week, it was baked in the hot summer sun, it was flung from trolley to Lost Property, and from Lost Property to guards' van. In the course of this (as we later discovered) the margarine melted and the lid came off the cocoa.

At Scout Meeting the week that the flag came back, we held a special ceremony in thanksgiving for a successful jamboree and the safe return of the Pope's special flag. The bugle blew, we all saluted and unfurled not the Papal colours of white and gold, but the flag of some obscure African Republic, (Lumbago perhaps?) brown on brown.

I left the hut that night and walked on civvy street, badgeless and broken, the rain mingling with the tears that were running down my cheeks: and I have never told anybody this before.

August, 2001.

Carry on up the Pole

It was 1976, the year of that scorching hot, never-ending summer when people were frying eggs on the pavements of Bradford, bacon on the pavements of Halifax, and meeting up in Cleckheaton for breakfast.

In a fit of madness I had decided to take the family and the dog and two additional small boys camping in Scotland. We were going to leave the Yorkshire Dales, head off for Galloway, spend a few days there, then head off up the coast taking ferries to Arran and Mull, ending our trip at Tobermory, proving to my children once and for all that it really was a place, and not a furry thing that collected rubbish on Wimbledon Common.

There was myself, Pat my wife, Sarah and Emma our daughters, who were ten and eleven, and David and John, Pat's brother and my brother respectively, who were roughly the same age as our daughters (don't ask – Catholic families were like that then).

And then there was Sam the Dog. Sam the Dog was an old English sheepdog who was really called Samantha and how I came to buy her from a Geordie herbal-cigarette-smoking sound engineer with one lung is another story all together. Sam could well have been the subject of somebody's PhD on bonding between the animal kingdom and the human race. She had been with us only a couple of years, but already thought she was human. I often used to drive with the girls on the back seat, Sam between them, and look in the driving mirror to see the dog sat up, carrying on a conversation with the girls in Growlish.

So there we all were, leaving Yorkshire in a Volvo estate car packed to the ashtray with clothes, food, walking gear, cooking stove, toys and books, maps, toilet rolls, plastic sick bags and two tents. One was the little two-man tent I'd used for most of my camping trips, the other was one of those huge canvas bungalows with parlours, vestibules, bedrooms and west wings. That was where the children and Sam were going to sleep. The big tent wasn't ours. It had been loaned us by a primary school teacher friend. I asked her if it was simple to put up.

'Dead easy,' she said. 'All the poles are coded.'

We reached the Solway Firth mid-afternoon. Salmon fishers were standing strung out across the river in chest waders, holding their nets up against the incoming tide. It looked a cold and boring job.

'Can't they afford a boat?' asked John.

'It's a traditional way of fishing,' I informed him.

'They're potty,' said Emma. And that was that.

We had afternoon tea at a small tea room, and rolled into The Isle of Whithorn just as the evening was settling in. There were several tents already pitched at the campsite, and men were sitting in deckchairs in the evening sun as we pulled on to our spot. The kids and the dog jumped out and began doing kids and dog things, and Pat and I started to put up the big tent.

We unpacked the bag that held the tent. All the three-piece poles once held together with springs had parted company from their springs, and were in pieces, so there seemed to be something like 50 bits of pole labelled, A3, A9, B9, P7, and so on, through numerous letters and dozens of numbers. I found out later that the lady who loaned us the tent had similarly labelled the hooks in the infants' cloakroom. For months infants had been going home with the wrong coats.

Presuming that Al joined to A2 we set to work. When all the poles were locked together we had something low and long that looked like the kind of tunnel lions run through on their way into the circus ring. The children and Sam would have had to sleep head-to-toe and crawl in backwards.

By now all the other campers on the site were sitting in deckchairs watching us. The children and Sam had given up playing and were watching too. This was much more fun. Sweating, and now raddled by the midges which had arrived as we opened the bag, we took it all apart and started again. The men smoked pipes to keep the midges away. We didn't have any pipes so we ripped up a pair of tights and pulled a leg each over our heads.

The midges went for our bare legs and arms. We flapped them away. Looking like bank robbers in khaki shorts with St Vitus Dance we set to work, coming out with all the swear words we knew under our breaths. Our second attempt was like Canary Wharfe; it stretched 50 feet up and would have meant the kids and Sam sleeping standing up on each other shoulders.

By now the men with pipes had all finished their dinner, and were smoking pipes again, while we were thinking about booking into a bed and breakfast. In a last desperate attempt I sorted all the poles out into sizes, and just sort of threw them together. Apart from the fact that the tent had a balcony, and the kids had to get in through a window, it was fine.

By now it was dark, and the men, realising that the performance had ended for the night, had gone to the pub. Dinner was jam sandwiches and a mug of cocoa, and we crawled exhausted into our respective pits.

Taking down the tent next morning gave me all the clues I needed. There were only three kinds of poles. Ridge, walls and apex. I bought three different coloured rolls of electrician's tape at the next town, colour coded the poles, and for the rest of the holiday it was all easy-peasey; a disappointment though for the men in pipes, who followed us to the next campsite hoping for another free show.

When I got back I showed our teacher friend how to write infants' names on bits of sticky paper. That worked too.

February, 2002.

Grumpy! Moi?

A zillion trillion curses on them! May they hobble backwards through Hell for God's life and a half with their plums on fire, and not a bucket of water for eternities! May they get the squint and the mange. May they marry their grandmothers, and the produce of the coupling be cats. May their willies fall off. May they be plagued by water filter salesmen for infinity. May they be riddled with boils, may the skies rain frogs on them, and may Icky the Bare Bum Fire Bobby find their address and come and sort them out.

Who? I hear you ask. And in a severe case of deja vu can I just say 4WD and Trial Riders – oh and the Railway and Bus People too – all of them, and all their kith, kin and progeny. I know that not too long ago I said something similar, but gentle reader, history has a way of repeating itself, and four wheel drive loonies and trial riders are breeding faster than rabbits. Let me explain. Last week on a glorious day of high summer I decided to leave Manchester, where I am at present domiciled, for a days hill walking in Ribblesdale.

It would be nice, I thought, to be able to leave the car behind and simply get the train to Settle, and set off from there. No chance. I pick up the phone and a nice lady in Calcutta tells me that to get to Settle from Manchester I would have to go to Leeds, going umpteen miles east to come all the way back again. But I can if I like go via Lancaster which means going umpteen miles north to change trains and then go south again. Both journeys will take something like three hours.

Stuff it thinks I. The bus will do. So I get on the computer, log on to the net and find the website of National Express. It comes up with a page of boxes. I have to type in the boxes where I want to go and where I want to go from, what date, how tall I am, whether I'm carrying any luggage, who is feeding the cats, what colour my mother's eyes are etc., etc. So I type in Manchester and Settle and (if you believe nothing else believe this – Communion's Honour) it comes up with the price and times of a journey from Manchester to Seville – only it's not available on the day I want to travel. I don't even try lastminute.com because the only time I ever looked at that site it was a dog's TV snack.

So I drove. Nothing else for it. An hour and a half later I have my boots on, my pack on my back, and I am following the old bridleway that leads from Helwith Bridge to Silverdale passing under the nose of Pen y Ghent. It was a glorious morning with the sun beating down and a light breeze cooling the dale; God is in her heaven and all is right with the world. Half a mile up the track I hear an engine. Farmer thinks I. No not farmer: two geeks in a brand new Range Rover playing at Daktari. I stand amazed watching them crawling noisily up the bridleway, over the hump below the mountain then off down into Silverdale. Ten minutes later nine goons on fart boxes arrive the same way clad all in leather and helmets, their engines loud, their exhausts stinking, ripping apart the silence and fouling the sweet air of that lovely summer's day. Call me an old spoil sport if you like but there are a couple of issues here.

Firstly being a bridleway the trail was legally open only to pedal cycles, walkers and horse riders, so that what they were doing was in effect illegal as they well knew: and secondly there comes a time when we have to ask ourselves whether the freedom to pursue our own particular foibles comes at the expense of other people's liberties. Not so long ago I used the freedom of this page to rail and rant against the people who see the great outdoors as something to drive across, and I fully expected the four wheel drive lobby and the trial riders to come down on me. Stupid of me. They ain't going to be reading this: they'll be reading *What Exhaust?* or *Differential and Helmet Monthly.* So much for the pen being mightier than the sword – that's only true if the pen is four feet long and the sword two inches.

So what happens next? Well I get to the top of the hill after a lovely scramble up the gritstone neb, and find a big lady on a mobile phone talking to somebody in Leeds.

'What's the weather like there. It's lovely here. Did you put the joint in? Have you let the cats out?'

Now call me an old spoil sport if you like, but had the nutters in the Range Rover come up the mountain and run over the lady on the mobile phone I would have seen it as some kind of justice, not poetic justice – that would have meant T. S. Eliot or Dylan Thomas driving the Range Rover, and they're both dead – but you know what I mean. There should be an island somewhere where mobile phone users, four wheel driver fanatics and trial riders can go and live and get up each others noses while microwaving their remaining brain cell. I don't know why I'm so nowty; I must be hormonal.

The rest of the day gentle reader was lovely. I wandered off down to Horton, had a pint mug of tea you could varnish a boat with, just the way tea should be, at the Pen y Ghent Café, and wobbled off back to Helwith Bridge by the river.

Oh, something did happen on the way back. As I was walking along this little used footpath I stumbled upon a couple who were as close to making the two backed beast as makes no difference. In the long grass of a hay meadow they were oblivious to the passing world, and were obviously having no trouble filling their day.

I passed by without peeping, and carried on my way thinking that I would rather the mountains were covered in couples *randy (as a biscuit* as my mate Tony calls it), than motorised loonies – the noise is minimal and the exhaust hardly noticeable.

July, 2000

Nostradamus on Ilkley Moor

I have to say this simply for good form's sake, even though this article was written before the Christmas deadline imposed by Macaroon Camiknickers, my Ubergruppenwritingfuhrer, and since then anything may have happened.

Happy New Year, if you are still out there, and we haven't all ascended into Heaven with the Doomsday Cults to sit at the right hand of a bloke with a beard. Likewise, if you aren't all down with the Millennium Bug, and if you aren't fighting off the ravaging hordes who have no water or electricity, and have taken time off from looting supermarkets to pay you a visit, then may I wish for you that your next thousand years be as happy and prosperous as the last thousand (always assuming of course that you aren't out there looting supermarkets yourselves).

So what will the next 2,000 years bring us walkers and climbers and ramblers and assorted outdoor types? Well I have chucked the old crystal ball under the stairs, and instead have logged on to the Internet, and downloaded the predictions on the Nostradamus Website (www.nostradamus.gloom.flood.fourhorsemen.plague.pyramid selling.com) and can report that the future looks interesting but glum.

It is the year 4,000, the Labour Party is still in power and still has not passed the Freedom to Roam Bill, which in any case is so watered down that it only applies on days when there is no hunting, and in months when there is no 'r' in the month.

The human race has evolved into an amoeba-like creature that can only breathe petrol and diesel fumes, after a thousand years of fast food, these blob-like organisms can only move with the aid of special powered Brasher boots. This means that all the major peaks in the world have been climbed by anybody who so wishes, using gas cylinders filled with traffic fumes, wearing thermal bubbles, and using the plasma-assisted Brasher Boots.

The first McDonald's has opened on Everest and another is planned for K2. Serving food made directly from petrochemical products, thereby cutting out any contact with the natural world (which is now preserved in seven bubble parks around the world), Big Everest Big Mac restaurant serves 200,000 customers in its first month. A Big Mac now costs £12m which is okay since the average worker makes £300m a week. World-wide, all poverty has been abolished since all the poor people have been eaten by the rich people.

Early on in the 21st century it was realised that landscape was really only useful if it had economic value. For the sake of future bio-developments, seven bubble parks were created worldwide in which curious and amazing ecosystems were preserved. These included the Mato Grosso in the Brazilian Amazon, the Everglades of Florida, the Gobi Desert and Hartlepool. The rest of the Earth's surface was covered with wind farms, car parks and executive homes, with the exception of those areas designated as *Fun Fun!! Amazing Theme Parks,* which included all the old National Parks of Europe and America, and anywhere else that Disneyworld Plc. Inc.com. bought, thinking it could make a buck. The Caledonian Disneyworld, with its Rob Roy Karaoke in the Clachaig Inn, and its real massacres (daily at 2 p.m. and 7 p.m. – allowing time for blood and limb clearance) are especially popular.

Sony/Toyota/Nissanland Plc. (formerly known as Australia) together with England Land Inc and the Top Of The Morning Begorrahland Eire Plc. have cancelled all trekking and hill-walking due to the popularity of virtual trekking with Surround Feel and Listen-0vision.

Trekking on the Moon, however, has become the new pastime of the rich and famous, and Plasma Brasher Boot Trekking on the Lunar McDonald's Trail has become very popular, particularly those treks led by the various Mallorys, Shiptons, Maurice Wilsons and Tillmans that are around, now that cloning from DNA has been perfected. Dozens of the great men have been created from traces of their DNA found on fountain pens, pipe stems the neck bands of their shirts, and (in the case of Wilson) from an old bra strap.

The Great Outdoors is still being published, beamed straight into people's brains from the mighty CalMag satellite. Its editor, Macaroon Camiknickers OBE, BEM, Inc. Com, has been cloned several times; the clones are all, variously, living in Auchtermuchty writing their memoirs, leading Virtual Reality Crews through Hindu Kush Funland, and promoting their own brand of single malt, the Maclivercrippler. Assistant editor John Manning has been stuck up an Irish Mountain with a gang of girl guides for centuries.

Seamus O'Perrin has discovered the secret of Eternal Life from a Guru on the summit of a Norfolk mountain, and has told everybody about it in his column. Unfortunately the mountain was destroyed during the building of the M3976, and the Guru is believed to be working cleaning car windscreens at some traffic lights somewhere.

The author of this book is long dead, having been assassinated on New Year's Day, 2001, by a group believed to have been led by the CLA and the Off Road Fun Drivers 4x4 Trail Bike Inc. Plc. Assoc. and Dierdre O'Hallorhan's mother.

January, 2000.

THE DIARY OF A YEOMANRY M.O.

(EGYPT, GALLIPOLI, PALESTINE AND ITALY)